Valued Friends

A play

Stephen Jeffreys

Samuel French - London
New York - Toronto - Hollywood

ISBN 0 573 01922 3

VALUED FRIENDS

First produced at the Hampstead Theatre, London, on
9th February, 1989, with the following cast of characters:

Sherry	Jane Horrocks
Howard	Peter Capaldi
Paul	Tim McInnerny
Marion	Serena Gordon
Scott	Martin Clunes
Stewart	Peter Caffrey

Directed by Robin Lefèvre

Designed by Sue Plummer

Lighting by Gerry Jenkinson

CHARACTERS

Sherry, late twenties
Howard, early thirties
Paul, early thirties
Marion, early thirties
Anthony Scott, thirty
Stewart, early forties

The action takes place in a sitting-room in the basement flat of a large, late-Victorian house in Earl's Court

Time—1984–1987

"An acre in Middlesex is better than a principality in Utopia."

Thomas Babington Macaulay

ACT I

SCENE 1

The sitting-room in the basement flat of a large, late-Victorian house in Earl's Court. Early June, 1984. Just before midnight

The room is cosy, carpeted and cluttered, with pictures on the walls. There are two doors, one to Paul and Marion's bedroom and one to the rest of the flat. There is also a pair of French windows with curtains, which look on to a small concrete garden

On one side of the room there is a fireplace with ornaments on the mantelpiece. Against the opposite wall there is a drinks cabinet and a radiator. There are several easy chairs, with an upright chair at the table. There is also a cassette machine. By the door to the hall there is a dimmer light switch

Music: "Needles and Pins" by the Searchers

The Lights come up on Howard sitting at his typewriter. He has commandeered the table and is surrounded by papers, books and card index systems

Sherry has just come in and is standing next to him. She wears a short dress, an absurd floppy hat and a huge shoulder bag

Sherry (*with great excitement and volume*) The train is packed Howard, I mean I've trodden on faces to get a seat. We're somewhere between Knightsbridge and South Kensington, there's this just incredible smell of sweat, you know, not stale sweat, excited summer sweat. Suddenly there's this guy, lurching towards me through the pack and he is *crazy*, there are no questions about this, the man is *gone* and he has singled out *me*, no-one else will do. He shoves aside the last remaining body and looms over me, hanging from the strap, swaying like a side of beef, I mean he's *enormous* and he starts stabbing his finger at me, "How much do you *care*? How much do you *care*?" That's all he's saying over and over. "How much do you *care*?" Everyone's looking at me. *He's* crazy but they're staring at *me*. They want to know how much I care too. About what, nobody's saying, so I take a chance, put my hand on my heart and say, "Very deeply, very deeply indeed," thinking this might get the crowd on my side, but no, nobody applauds, nobody cries, nobody even *laughs*. They're just waiting for the crazy to come back at me, and, Howard, he does. "What about? What do you care so much about?" And they all *stare* at me again. I can feel the mood of the train switching against me. We get to South Ken but nobody gets off. They all live there, I know they do, but they're saying to themselves, "We'll walk back from Gloucester

Road." The doors shut, the train starts. "What about? What do you care *about*?" Howard, I can't think of anything. In a calmer moment I might have said, "The early films of Ingmar Bergman, my mum and being the greatest stand-up comedian the world has ever seen." But I can think of *nothing*. The silence is just incredible. I mean I'm not ignoring the guy, I'm racking my brains. The whole carriage is racking my brains. Eventually I look the guy in the face, admission of defeat, and he just says, "You see, you see." And the doors open and he gets off at Gloucester Road. All those people who really live in South Ken are now saying to themselves "What a glorious evening—we'll walk back from Earl's Court." Howard, they're prepared to stay on till Hounslow Central, gawping at my embarrassment. We get to Earl's Court, I'm so paranoid I can't face them all in the lift, I have to climb the emergency stairs to escape. Have you *any* idea how many emergency stairs there are at Earl's Court?

Howard Eighty-four.

Sherry Are there really?

Howard I counted them.

Sherry What a nightmare. Are you going to make some tea?

Howard No.

Sherry I put the kettle on when I came in.

Howard I don't want any tea.

Sherry Oh. Did you go out collecting tonight?

Howard They phoned me up. I told them I was ill.

Sherry Howard!

Howard I've been out twice. What's the point? Collecting for the miners in the Royal Borough of Kensington and Chelsea? I was stood two hours outside the tube on Monday with me plastic bucket, copped one pound forty and I put the quid in meself. If I'd been up in Glasgow I'd not have been able to hold the thing up after five minutes.

Sherry So you're writing the book instead?

Howard That's it.

Sherry Going well?

Howard No.

Sherry Oh.

There is a pause

Are the others in?

Howard I'm sorry.

Sherry No. I didn't mean you were being——

Howard I'm just tired, I'd like to go to bed.

Sherry —boring or anything. Well go to bed.

Howard I can't, I need to speak to Paul and Marion.

Sherry Where've they gone?

Howard Concert. The Searchers.

Sherry Oh yeah. More sixties nostalgia. Is it healthy I ask? I mean, you can't imagine these destruction metal bands getting together for twenty-first anniversary gigs.

Howard Destruction metal?

Sherry Very big in Germany. These guys, they hire a warehouse and smash the stage up with drills and amplified sledgehammers. It's pretty loud. Paul did a piece about it in the *NME*.

Howard You mean, they use, like, manufacturing tools for——

Sherry Yeah, cement mixers and stuff——

Howard —signalling the decline of manufacturing culture, that's ... (*He makes a note*)

Sherry Apparently it gets pretty dangerous. I mean you're standing there listening and the walls fall in on you, it's meant to be great.

Howard Well it would be.

Sherry You gonna put that in your book?

Howard Might make a nice little footnote. The section on de-industrialization.

Sherry Howard. You couldn't lend me some money, could you?

There is a pause

Howard How much d'you want?

Sherry Just—a tenner. Is that all right? Brian at the *Queen's Head* owes me for my last three gigs—and he wasn't around tonight, bastard, and there's a few——

Howard I'll lend you ten quid, Sherry. (*He reaches in his pocket*)

There is the sound of people arriving through the front door

Did it go all right, the *Queen's Head*?

Sherry Pretty dead audience. Got a couple of laughs towards the end. I don't think they understood what I was doing at all.

Howard hands her a ten pound note

Oh ... that's great, ta.

Howard Well as long as you're getting the bookings, getting the experience.

Sherry Yeah, well. I'm getting the experience. But the audiences don't seem to be learning much from it.

Sherry scrunches the money up and hides it in her hand as she hears Paul and Marion approach the sitting-room

Paul enters, carrying his car keys in his hand

Marion closely follows him

Paul You're still up.

Marion They're still up.

Howard Good were they?

Paul Merely stunning.

Sherry Didn't get their pacemakers wired up in their wah-wah pedals, then——

Paul It's easy to be cynical. They did not look one day older. Twenty-two years on the road and they looked like a set of fresh-faced youths.

Marion And they hadn't learned any new songs either.

Paul You know what I admire? I admire the sheer stamina, the slog, the perseverance. All this bullshit you hear about the rock 'n' roll heroes, the ones who destroy themselves with drugs, or chuck lawsuits at each other or get killed in plane crashes. That's not heroic, that's the soft option. You know what true heroism is? It's twenty-two years in a Ford Transit staring at the cat's eye lights on the way back from the Club-a-Go-Go, Lowestoft.

Marion Does anyone want tea?

Howard Love some.

Sherry It's just boiled, I put it on.

Marion My ears are ringing. (*She turns to go*)

Sherry (*following her*) Marion. I had this really weird thing happened to me on the tube. There we were between Knightsbridge and South Ken . . .

Marion and Sherry exit

Paul (*holding up a cassette*) Look at that, eh, magnetic gold.

Howard You got an interview?

Paul Fifteen minutes' worth. Frank and John. Classic. Cut some old favourites into it and I've got a nifty programme. Syndicate it globally. (*He slumps into a chair*)

Howard tidies some papers

(*Suddenly remembering*) And! And—you'll never guess.

Howard What?

Paul The support band.

Howard The Swinging Blue Jeans.

Paul More obscure.

Howard The Downliners Sect?

Paul More talentless.

Howard More talentless than the Downliners Sect? I give in.

Paul The Blue Scarecrows.

Howard Never heard of them.

Paul You won't have heard of them. They've only been together for six months. But you will have heard of the bass guitarist.

Howard Jack Bruce down on his luck, is he?

Paul Dennis Combes.

Howard Never.

Paul The man himself.

Howard Dennis Combes.

Paul Bass guitar, vocals and insulting the audience.

Howard Making a go of it then, is he?

Paul No. Had a few words with him. Christine—remember Christine—they're married now, just about—she's got a good job, likes to get him out of the house of an evening.

Howard Can see her point. Was he good?

Paul Same as ever. Played a fretless. Still trying to sound like Charlie Mingus.

Howard He was all right, Dennis. The two of you were good together.

Paul Well . . .

Howard You were, should have stuck at it.

Paul Like The Searchers.

Howard Could have been where they are today.

Paul The thing with Dennis, the real problem, was that he never accepted the idea that the bass guitar is a background instrument. There you are, up on the stage singing the crucial line of the lyric, and Dennis turns up his amp and starts playing semi-tone runs, crawling up and down the fingerboard like a demented spider.

Howard Great days. Remember the big gig. The Old Refectory.

Paul I've still got the ticket. It was pink. October the twenty-seventh, nineteen seventy-three Southampton University's own band, Centrifugal Force, supporting Leonard Cohen.

Howard Shrewd piece of booking. Everyone cheered up when Leonard came on, he seemed quite chirpy in comparison.

Paul Lennie Cohen. Remember how old we thought he looked.

Howard Great days.

Paul Great days. Old Dennis.

Howard You were mad to jack it in.

Paul I still play——

Howard You know, in a *band*. I reckon if you'd have stuck at it you could really have——

Paul Yeah, shut up, will you Howard. (*Pause*) Interviewing Bronski Beat for the *NME* tomorrow.

Howard Oh yeah?

Paul Oh *yeah*.

Marion and Sherry enter

Marion is carrying a tray with a traditional earthenware teapot, four distinctive mugs, a bottle of milk, a sugar bowl and a packet of biscuits on it

Sherry (*continuing her previous conversation*) ... all those people who actually live in South Ken have decided, "What a stupendous evening, we'll walk back from Earl's Court," I mean, they're prepared to walk back from——

Howard Hounslow Central.

Sherry Howard——

Paul What's this?

Sherry I was telling Marion——

Howard She had to climb the emergency stairs by all accounts——

Sherry Shut up, Howard——

Paul Will somebody tell me——

Sherry This guy I met, on the train between——

Howard (*suddenly standing up*) Look, I want to go to bed.

Paul, Sherry and Marion are puzzled by his vehemence

There is a pause

Paul Well go to bed then.

Howard sits down again

Howard I waited up to tell you something. Some news. It affects all of us. I thought I should wait until we were all together.

Marion pours the tea and hands it round

Marion If we've got mice again, I'm leaving.
Howard We've got a new landlord.

There is a pause

Paul Is that it?
Sherry We're always having new landlords.
Paul Seven in ten years.
Sherry Eight now.
Paul Yeah, eight now.
Howard The rumour is, this one's different.
Paul Says who?
Howard Tracey from the top flat. She came down earlier on, asked if I'd heard anything.
Paul And?
Howard Well I said no, and Tracey said the guy on the second floor, the bald geezer——
Paul —the one with the Renault Five——
Howard Yeah, he'd gone, cleared off 'cos the landlord had found something dodgy in his lease, and he'd said that the people on the ground floor had been offered three grand each to leave.
Sherry Three thousand pounds, just to clear off?
Howard That's the story.
Paul And is that the lot?
Howard So far.

There is a pause

Paul Tracey says that the bald Renault driver, now departed, says that the ground floor have been offered three grand each to go. It's not exactly Reuters we've got here, Howie.
Howard All right, next time I'll keep it to myself.
Sherry Three thousand pounds. Be handy, wouldn't it?

Howard, Paul and Marion look at her doubtfully

Paul We had the same story, exactly the same, two years ago when that Swedish woman sold out.

Howard stands

Howard OK. OK. Sorry I mentioned it. I can go to bed now. Sorry it wasn't more interesting. Put my tea on the side and I'll heat it up for breakfast. Good-night.

Howard exits

Sherry Good-night.

Paul goes to the door, looks, then follows Howard

Paul (*off*) Howie!!
Sherry Marion?
Marion Yes?
Sherry You couldn't lend me ten quid, could you?
Marion Ummm . . . ohhh . . . I expect so.
Sherry It's just that Brian, the bastard owes me——
Marion You know we've got to pay the phone bill this week.
Sherry Is it a lot?
Marion Well. Your share is.
Sherry Oh shit.
Marion Paul's worked it out. It's on the hall table.
Sherry Oh. (*Pause*) I'd still like ten quid.
Marion Tomorrow?
Sherry That would be—lovely, yes.
Marion I suppose it must end somehow. Why not like this?
Sherry What?
Marion Living together. It's been ten years. Life's not meant to happen that
   way. After a while you go your separate ways, buy squeaky clean places
   with freezers and get surrounded by cats and children. I've met people
   who've done it.
Sherry Well, this might be your chance. You could go and do all that with
   Paul.
Marion Would he want that?
Sherry Probably. I know he likes freezers.
Marion Would I want that?
Sherry Yes, I should think so.
Marion And what would you do?
Sherry Kip on floors, I don't know.
Marion You're getting a bit big for that, Sherry. Floors, that was a long
   time ago.

Paul enters

Paul He's all right. He was just pissed off cos he's got to get up early to pick
   up some leaflets at the printers for his NATFHE branch.
Sherry It was silly staying up. I don't see why he didn't get me to tell you.
Paul Did you see the breakdown of the phone bill?
Sherry No I haven't. Stop hounding me.
Paul It's the first time I've mentioned it.
Sherry It's always money now. You used to be able to get some really good
   conversation in this flat. Burning issues and moral dilemmas and things.
   Now all everyone talks about is money.
Marion I should get time to go to the bank at lunchtime.
Sherry Sorry? Oh right. The money. (*She gets up and heads for the door*) See
   you in the morning.

Sherry exits

Paul What money?
Marion She's broke.

Paul You shouldn't lend to her, it makes her worse.

Marion I said I was going to read those reports for Jeremy tonight, oh well.

Paul Picks up forty quid a week if she's lucky, then splurges out eighty in the Portobello Road on an antique wedding dress that doesn't fit her.

Marion She'd be happy. If we got money to go.

Paul Don't talk about it or she'll spend all the cash on the offchance.

Marion I was talking to Jackie today. Marketing Jackie. She hadn't realized how old I was. She thought I was about twenty-five. She went all quiet.

Paul Even if it did happen and the landlord came up with a heap of money I still wouldn't go. It's ideal, living here.

Marion Marketing's funny. They all sit round and say things like "In five years time, every home will have a computer like every home has a toaster."

Paul What happened to our toaster?

Marion It broke.

Paul You don't look thirty-one. Twenty-six, twenty-seven at the outside.

Marion bends over and kisses him

Marion I'm going to bed. Jennifer's having a baby.

Paul Jennifer.

Marion Roger and Jennifer.

Paul Oh.

Marion We could buy a place. If he came up with enough.

Paul The four of us?

Marion No, silly, you and me. Renting doesn't make sense.

Paul We've been renting for years. When did it stop making sense?

Marion Sometimes it feels a bit cramped. Anyway, everything changes eventually.

Paul I don't like change. I like things that go on and on.

Marion breaks away from him and goes towards the bedroom door

Marion?

Marion Bring me a glass of water when you come, will you?

Marion exits into the bedroom

Paul sits for a moment. Then he remembers the interview tape. He gets up and puts it in the cassette machine. He goes to the drinks cupboard and pours a brandy

Paul's voice is heard on the tape

Paul I'm backstage at the Albany Empire, Deptford after a tremendous gig by that great band of the sixties and indeed the eighties, the Searchers, and I've got bass guitarist Frank Allen with me. Frank, you've got that distinctive Searchers sound, I mean the high harmonies and twelve string guitars, that's had quite an impact on rock and roll history.

Frank It has, I mean the Byrds got a lot of credit for that, but in fact the Byrds used the twelve string sometime after us and I believe they were influenced, certainly Tom Petty has admitted being influenced by our twelve string sound and Bruce Springsteen. He was using "When You Walk in the Room" on his stage show for quite some time. And Marshall Crenshaw came to see us in New York . . .

Quick fade to Black-out

Music: "When You Walk in the Room" by the Searchers

SCENE 2

The same. Evening. December, 1984

The room is much tidier. Christmas cards adorn every available surface. There is a small, genuine Christmas tree with working lights

Marion is hoovering. She is wearing a suit and gives the impression of being older and richer than she really is

She switches the hoover off, and looks around, houseproud

Paul enters. He is clearly anxious

Paul Are we going to offer him a drink?
Marion No.
Paul Are you sure?
Marion We want him in and out quickly. We want to make him feel like an intruder. We want tension and hostility.
Paul So no drinks, not even coffee.
Marion Not even coffee.
Paul It's cold out there, he'll be cold.
Marion The psychology is: no coffee.
Paul Right.

There is a pause

They're not going to get here in time. I knew we should have made it later.
Marion It doesn't matter.
Paul It does matter. We don't want Howard lecturing him on economics and we don't want Sherry saying anything.

There is the sound of the front door opening and closing

Marion I talked to them last night. They know what to do.

Sherry enters, running. She is wearing a heavy coat

Sherry Oh God. He's not here yet.
Marion No.
Sherry Christ it's so cold. (*She goes to the drinks cupboard and pours herself a large brandy*)

Paul is stupefied by Sherry's actions

I had this really amazing thing happen to me on the bus——

Marion Not now. You know what to do?

Sherry Yes, I say nothing. Absolutely nothing. I leave it to the smooth-tongued among us. When he speaks to me I say, "Signor Landlord, I know nothing, nada, absoluto zilcho——"

Paul Do you often drink my brandy?

Sherry What?

Paul Elton John's manager gave me that.

Sherry Paul, it's really cold outside, you have no idea——

Paul If it's my birthday. Or I have something to celebrate. Or I'm in the depths of terminal depression. Then I have some of my cognac——

Marion Please.

Paul Then and only then——

Sherry It's only a drink——

Paul If you just wanna get warm, there's a bottle of sherry I got off Bananarama——

Marion Please!

There is a pause

He'll be here any second. Howard will probably be late. The important thing is this: we will give away nothing, no information at all. Our financial standing, our mutual relationships, our careers, these will remain a closed book to him, all right? He's the landlord, make him feel like one. If there's any official statement required from our side, Paul will make it and there will be no dissenters, right?

Sherry Right.

Marion And above all: if he mentions a sum of money, whatever it is, as compensation for our giving him vacant possession, we look incredibly depressed.

Sherry Depressed, right.

There is a ring at the doorbell

Sherry Oh shitbags.

Marion I'll go. (*She makes for the door, then turns for a moment*) Sit down. Looks as if you live here.

Marion exits

Paul and Sherry sit

Sherry Suppose he offers us the four grand Tracey and the others got——

Paul You look depressed——

Sherry I'll try——

There is a pause

Paul Think of something to say——

Sherry I can't——

Paul Quick before he comes in——

Sherry Oh Christ, oh internal megadeath——

Marion enters

Anthony Scott follows her. He is a go-getter, only just thirty, younger than the inhabitants of the flat though he doesn't realize this. He has a public school manner, and he is clean, clear-cut, confident. Despite themselves, Paul and Sherry stand when Scott comes in. Scott holds some papers, recently extracted from his briefcase. He is talking into a micro tape recorder as he comes in

Scott ... substantial areas of wasted space, corridors and so on, then large reception room, French windows, opening to garden, rear, good-evening, so you two are ...

Scott looks at Sherry and checks his papers

Sherry does not know if she should speak

Paul Paul Cameron.
Scott Excellent. Anthony Scott.

Scott and Paul shake hands

So therefore, the other one's called Howard, you must be Sherry Martin.

Sherry is immensely relieved

Sherry Yes, pleased to meet you.

Sherry and Scott shake hands

Although my equity name is Sherry St George.

Paul and Marion look appalled

Scott (*puzzled*) Equity? Do you deal?
Sherry It's just you can't have the same name as somebody else, and somebody else already had my name, although—obviously it *was* her name, so I had to find another and my aunt's maiden name was St George so I thought—rather stylish and ...

Scott looks at her as if she were mad

As a stage name ...
Scott *That* Equity. Sorry didn't cotton. Different worlds. (*He sits down*) Are you all in that line of business?
Sherry No, Paul's a freelance broadcaster and Marion's in computers. Howard's not here yet, he's a lecturer at ... (*She realizes she has said too much*) ... the moment. That's why he's not here yet. (*She pauses*)

Paul and Marion look daggers at Sherry

But he'll be here soon. When he finishes his lecture. (*She pauses*) It's about the re-birth of German industry in the nineteen fifties. (*She pauses*) So he won't be long. Can I make you a cup of coffee?
Scott I—no I really mustn't stay long. Should we wait for this——
Paul Howard. Howard Unwin.
Scott Perhaps we'll give him a moment or so. You're an actress then?
Sherry Well I'm more of a performer, really. I'm breaking into the alternative comedy scene.

There is the sound of the front door opening and closing

Scott Television? Lots of money in that.
Sherry Yes. On a good night, you can take home twenty quid.
Scott Ah.

Howard enters

Howard Sorry I'm late. Howard Unwin.
Scott Anthony Scott.

Scott and Howard shake hands

For a man who's had to explain an economic miracle, I'd say you were a shade early.

Howard can't work out how Scott knows

The Krauts, your lecture. Lot to learn from them.
Howard Well, yes.

Howard searches the faces around him for clues

(*Giving up*) I'll sit down.

Scott immediately leans forward. He is well prepared

Scott (*in a cards-on-the-table-manner*) Now you've been living here as tenants for quite some time, five years, isn't that right?
Paul Ten.
Scott Ten. (*He seems momentarily depressed*) Long time. Well. You will not be unaware of the situation. My line of business is property. My interest is primarily, I would say, a creative one. I like to seize opportunities and make the most of them. Six months ago I bought this property as part of a portfolio of similar—units. You'll be aware I bought it sight unseen, tenants and all because I have a particular interest in the area and . . . Well a good price is a good price.

There is a pause

I should, perhaps, apologize for having taken so long to contact you, but I was aware you were tenants of long standing and I decided to—approach the other occupants first. Now, you're here in the basement. The second floor and the ground floor are both vacant. The top floor will be vacant by the end of January, the first floor by the sixteenth of February. You will be the sole remaining tenants. I want to be quite clear about this, I have no intention of being a landlord. That's not my—thing at all. I—that is my company Anthony Scott Developments—refurbish properties—substantial buildings in promising locations renovated with a degree of wit and imagination—and then sold. To an increasingly clamorous market. Earls Court—becoming an interesting part of the world. Conservation area, nice London square, convenient for the city, handy for the airport, lots of brownie points . . . (*He looks around*) Needs a bit of work. As with much rented accommodation, the landlord tends to let things slip. Actually, needs an awful lot of work.

There is a pause

What I'd like to do is gut the whole house, shove in a central wall, re-arrange the accommodation on to different levels, so you have seven or eight different units, one bedroom, two bedroom flats, making the whole property more space efficient.

Paul They did that to the one on the corner.
Howard Yes they did, they put in a——
Paul Central wall, yes.
Scott Yes.

There is a pause

This work will be much easier to accomplish if you are no longer living here.

There is a pause

So. There are a number of routes available. A number of routes. All of which we are at liberty to explore. One of which we will choose to travel on.

There is a pause

Route one, and this is the route I absolutely prefer and which I cannot recommend to you too highly ... I will pay you a sum of money for vacant possession. Which you would dispose amongst yourselves as you thought fit. And we would name a date for your vacation of the premises. (*He looks around*)

Sherry, Paul, Howard and Marion look back at him

Should we—for any reason—not be able to avail ourselves of this route, then we may have to get into re-housing. This could be rather a messy route. Under the terms of your tenancy, I would need to find accommodation of an equivalent nature to that which you are now enjoying. Now obviously it can't be *exactly* the same and we might find ourselves quibbling over a French window here and a lavatory pedestal there—if you catch my ... it's a bit wrangly, a bit nit-picky as processes go, which is why I'm not madly keen to set foot down this particular ... boulevard. But of course if we can't agree on option one, then re-housing it may have to be. I may not be into being landlord, but I have a colleague who is and he has a whole *sea* of flats not a biscuit's toss from this very spot and, should it come to the push, I have little doubt that the courts will rule one of these to be as damn near equivalent as equivalent can be ...

Scott waits for some comment, but there are still no takers

Failing that, I could in the very near future turn this place into a building site. A lot of work could be done around you, scaffolding, brickdust, rough labouring chaps working funny hours with their jovial badinage floating in through the windows—and in the meantime I can hardly fail to note that the rent you're paying is way below the going whack for this area. If I were to make a concerted push at the Rent Tribunal to bring you into line, you could well find yourself paying twice or thrice the current sum. But this is not a pleasant option, not by any means a scenic route. It's possible that we'll have no problems whatever reaching an agreement, in which event, it may be possible for me to offer you one of the newly created units on this very spot in the not too distant future, possibly at a highly competitive price. So. That's it.

There is a pause

That's where we stand.

There is a pause

Paul You mentioned a sum of money.
Scott Yes.
Paul For vacant possession.
Scott Yes.
Paul What sort of sum are we talking about?
Scott Well, this would be a figure on which we would have to agree.

Paul, Howard, Sherry and Marion wait

But I would have to say, at this juncture, that the absolute ceiling on such a sum, working as I am within tight budgets, the absolute ceiling would be around twenty thousand, twenty-five thousand, say around six thousand each.

Marion, Paul and Howard instantly look incredibly depressed

Sherry (*a yelp of joy*) Yahhh!! (*Suddenly she realizes she has to suppress her feelings*) Well, that's not very . . . I mean that's . . . well . . . as a sum . . . that's . . .

There is a pause

Scott And I think I ought to say, right from the start, that we are not in a negotiating situation here. You are not about to make a killing out of me. We are not talking telephone numbers. We will be looking to settle amicably, speedily and sensibly.

There is a pause

Paul Well we obviously can't make any decision here and now. We'll need to consult among ourselves——
Scott Surely, surely.
Paul There is one point I would very much like to make. This is our home. It has been our home for some considerable time. We would none of us be at all happy to have to leave it.
Scott Well, this is a point of view, yes. But the world moves on, times change and so forth——
Paul It's a pleasant area, convenient for all our working arrangements, we get on extraordinarily well together, almost like a family——
Scott (*becoming embarrassed and making up his mind to get out*) Well. (*Looks at his watch*) I have to be going. I have another . . . (*He leans*

forward) I think you should talk through this very clearly amongst yourselves.

Scott searches for a possible ally and fixes on Sherry

I would greatly appreciate an early response. (*He stands*) Look, what are we now, the fifteenth of December. If you can give me vacant possession by the ... fifteenth of February, I shall pay you thirty thousand pounds. Thirty thousand. All right. And I think you can consider yourselves damn lucky.

Scott hands Sherry a business card

Telephone me. In a few days. When you've talked.

Scott exits

Marion follows him out

Sherry is about to let out a whoop of joy, but Paul claps his hand over her mouth at the last moment

Howard (*monitoring Scott's progress along the corridor*) They're passing the phone now, just edging into the kitchen, up to the fridge, past the fridge, he's lingering there in the doorway, a quick word, another quick word and he's—*gone!*

Paul removes his hand from Sherry's mouth

Sherry Thirty thousand! Thirty thousand pounds, yeah! (*Pause*) How much is that each?
Paul You're getting nothing.
Sherry No really——
Howard Seven thousand five hundred—
Sherry Seven thousand five hundred! Pounds!
Paul Sherry——
Sherry Yes, I know, I know——
Paul I mean, you all but screwed up the whole thing—

Marion enters

Marion Could you, I ask myself, have managed to divulge more information?
Sherry I'm sorry——
Marion I seriously doubt it——
Howard All that about Germany, how did he know that——
Paul Sherry broke down under questioning——
Sherry I know, I'm sorry, I'm sorry, I just got unnerved by the quiet, but we got the result, eh? Seven and a half thousand each!

Marion, Howard and Paul look at Sherry

Paul Well. It's not a bad starting point.
Howard He was definitely worried by the end——
Sherry Starting point? But he said—didn't he—that to get the money we had to be out by—when was it?

Howard The fifteenth of February.

Sherry Right, otherwise the offer would be off, that's what I thought.

Paul Well he would say that, wouldn't he?

There is a pause

Sherry You mean ... we're not going to take it? (*She looks at all of them, then sits despondent*) We're not going to take it, are we?

Paul (*explaining*) *We* are holding all the cards. *He* is setting up an artificial deadline in order to panic us into a decision. *We* are not going to be panicked.

Marion Just look how much it went up just by sitting here staring at him. He started at twenty. We made ten grand in five minutes just by keeping our mouths shut.

Howard Paul was magnificent. All that sob story stuff——

Marion "Our lovely home."

Howard "Couldn't bear to leave it——"

Marion "One big happy family."

Marion and Howard are in a great state of mirth

Paul (*a little puzzled*) Well. It is a nice flat, isn't it? We do like living here.

There is a slight pause

Howard Sure, yes, it was just, I mean the way you said it, sort of laid on with a trowel——

Sherry But look, he pointed out, you know, all the things he could do—turn it into a building site——

Paul Oh balls——

Sherry Put the rent up——

Howard In point of fact, the rent, because it's a controlled rent, can only go up by small increments. Even if he argues to the Tribunal that the facilities here have been vastly improved, which quite patently they haven't—

No-one is listening to Howard

Paul He can't turn it into a building site, because if we're still here, he can't develop it. The guy actually said, he wanted to put in a central wall——

Sherry So what are we doing? We're not taking the money, what are we doing?

Paul We're going to sit it out, we're going to stay here until he pays us a decent price.

Sherry You mean, even more than thirty thousand ...

Paul Sherry, think it through. You're given seven and a half grand. You're out on the street, what do you do?

Sherry Take a taxi to the Ritz.

Paul If we play our cards right, we could get enough out of him to buy a place.

Sherry What, the four of us?

Paul Well. Not necessarily the four of us. But—some of us—at the end of this process—should be in a position to buy ...

There is a pause

Sherry All right then. We're not taking thirty thousand. We're going to sit here, getting in Scott's way. So when does it stop? What do we take?

Howard I don't see that we have to put a figure on it. I mean, we're in the basement, so we're in possession of the drains, now the drains, it seems to me are a key feature if you're wanting to make dinky flatlets of the whole——

Marion Sixty thousand.

There is a pause

That's what we want. Fifteen thousand each. The golden rule when dealing with these people is to take the first sum they offer you and double it. So. He offers us seven and a half each. I personally will not move from this place until I have a cheque for fifteen thousand pounds in my hot little hand.

There is a pause

Sherry (*disbelieving*) Fifteen thousand? Each?

Paul She's right. Aim high. It's there for the taking.

Marion Howard?

Howard Well, I think the principle is—right, I'd put it, in practical terms just a shade lower, you know, maybe forty, forty-five . . .

Sherry Supposing he tries to re-house us.

Paul We keep objecting. It has to be equivalent accommodation. We just keep saying . . .

Marion The kitchen's smaller . . .

Paul It's further from the tube . . .

Marion The rent's higher . . .

Paul He won't want to take us to court. He wouldn't want the hassle.

There is a pause

Sherry So we just sit. Until he offers us . . . sixty thousand.

Marion That's it.

Howard And if he doesn't?

Marion Then we just . . . sit. Until he does.

Quick fade to Black-out

Music: "I Don't Like Mondays" by the Boomtown Rats

SCENE 3

The same. July, 1985

Some of the books, ornaments and pictures are now missing. They have been packed into the cardboard boxes which stand prominently in a corner

Paul is sitting at the table

Paul (*speaking clearly into a good quality microphone*) . . . but now standing here in the vast emptiness of Wembley Stadium, it seems impossible to believe that in a few days time, Bob Geldof's dream will be transformed into reality.

Sherry enters then, seeing Paul recording, stops in her tracks, trying to look unobtrusive

Before my eyes, teams of blue-overalled workmen are just starting to assemble ton upon ton of scaffolding . . .

Sherry looks perplexed

. . . into the enormous stage which will be graced on Saturday by some of the most prestigious names in rock music today. And the giant video screen, at present just a skeletal framework, will be carrying images, not only of the super-celebrities who are to perform here, but also of the silent millions on whose behalf they will play. This is Paul Cameron from Wembley Stadium for the ABC. (*Pause*) This is Paul Cameron from Wembley Stadium for Radio Free Europe. (*Pause*) This is Paul Cameron from Wembley Stadium for RTE (*Pause*) This is Paul Cameron from Wembley Stadium for Radio Zagreb. (*He switches the tape off*)

Sherry You certainly get around.

Paul The tapes get around. I'm always stuck here.

Sherry Is Howard in?

Paul No.

Sherry You said you were going to record my act and put it in a piece on the alternative comedy scene.

Paul Sherry, this stuff goes out to Tasmania and Warsaw and places. It won't increase the audience for your three minutes of random obscenity at the *Queen's Head* on a Sunday night.

Sherry Be nice to have a reputation, even if it's only an international one. (*She makes to go*)

Paul Sherry. What do you want to do?

Sherry I don't know.

Paul Somehow we've got to find a way out of the deadlock.

Sherry I would love to find a way out of the deadlock. Only I don't seem to have much clout around here. Marion makes up her mind what she wants, you go along with her because you're a couple, and Howard goes along with you so he can be in a majority. It doesn't seem to matter much what I think.

Paul OK, I see that. Now tell me what you want to do?

Sherry In an ideal world?

Paul In an ideal world.

Sherry OK, I would like all this to end. Just stop. I would like Anthony Scott's scaffolding and rubble and workmen to disappear. I would like to be able to answer the phone without the fear of him shouting at me and calling us a lot of bastard ingrates. I would like it very much if other people stopped packing my belongings into cardboard boxes just to give Scott the impression that we're actually about to move. And—yes, I would like Marion to stop screaming "Fifteen thousand each or die" every time I try to discuss the situation. (*She has made herself quite upset*) Paul, I just want to take the ten thousand Scott's offered and go. And I honestly don't care what happens afterwards.

There is a pause

Paul Right. OK. I understand that.

Sherry Now. You tell me what you want. Not Marion, *you*.

Paul I want to stay here——

Sherry Paul, we can't stay here, that's the whole——

Paul And Marion would like to have some children.

Sherry I know that, I didn't ask about that——

Paul But it's relevant. Marion would like us to buy a place together and have children——

Sherry Well, I don't see why you don't do just that. You'll have ten grand each, that's plenty, she's just got promoted, what's all the fuss about the extra five grand? Take the money and breed.

Paul Ah, well. There's one problem we have here. And it's rather a large one.

There is a pause

Marion and I are no longer a couple. Any more. Which I—regret. We may look like a couple. On account of sleeping in the same bed. But that's a matter of convenience. We have to do that until we get Scott's money. And when we do, we're going our separate ways.

There is a pause

Sherry Everybody knows this, don't they.

There is a pause

Everybody knows this except me.

Paul Who's everybody? I know obviously. Marion knows.

Sherry Howard?

Paul Well, Howard knows, but Marion doesn't know that Howard knows.

Sherry You told Howard.

Paul Yes.

Sherry On account of Howard being a boy and boys talk to boys.

Paul I suppose.

Sherry Then how come girls haven't talked to girls. Girls always talk to girls.

Paul Well I suppose ... Marion at the moment is ...

Sherry I get it. She wants the two of you to look like a united front. If I'm kept in ignorance then there's less chance of me thinking I can scream the place down for taking the ten thousand and going.

Paul Well now you know.

Sherry This is awful. When you started going out together, she cycled four miles to tell me. What's happened, Paul I don't understand.

Paul It's a perfectly rational decision. She wants to have children. And I don't. That's the way it's always been. But I thought I'd wear her down and she thought she'd wear me down. After ten years the contest has been declared a draw. It's obvious. She hasn't that much more time. Like I said, it's perfectly rational.

Sherry That's why she needs fifteen grand instead of ten. 'Cos she's going it alone.

Paul That's right. She's seen exactly the sort of place she wants. She's done the sums. It's very tight. She's made up her mind.

Sherry I haven't even thought. I'd pack and leave in an hour if I could and I haven't given a thought to where I'd go.

Paul Well. Perhaps it's time you did. How would you like to buy a flat with me and Howard?

Sherry Would I have to have children?

Paul Children do not figure in this particular deal.

Sherry That's something. A flat? You're crazy, with you and Howard? I haven't got any money, Paul, that's the whole point.

Paul Not any old flat. This flat. And you have got money. You're about to get x thousand pounds from Anthony Scott where x is a number between ten and fifteen.

Sherry But—if we buy this flat, then we can't be leaving it. And if we're not leaving it, then we won't be getting the money.

Paul Exactly. In this scenario, the money you would get from Scott would be theoretical money.

There is a pause

Sherry looks confused

Scott phoned at seven a.m. yesterday. While he was out jogging. We had a lunchtime meeting. He's had to alter all his plans. Because of us. There'll be no central wall, no clusters of dinky flatlets. He just wants shot of the place. He's lined up buyers for the other four flats. As they are. He should worry. With the price boom, he'll still make two hundred grand. Just over a year, not bad. So. This flat is now valued at ninety-five, his figure. We can either take the forty grand between us to go. Or we can buy the flat at the knock-down price of fifty grand. See, he either gives us forty thousand in real money or forty-five thousand in theoretical money.

Sherry So you, me and Howard buy. What happens to Marion? Some of the theoretical money should be hers.

Paul Precisely. My plan is this: the three of us buy the flat for fifty. Seventeenish each. Then we pay Marion fifteen to go. And everyone's happy.

Sherry Marion gets fifteen grand?

Paul From you, me and Howard. Five each. It's a bit unfair but it gets a result.

Sherry So what you're saying is instead of someone giving me a cheque for ten thousand pounds, you want me to give two other people cheques to the value of—twenty-one thousand pounds.

Paul Call it twenty-three with extras.

Sherry And you actually think this is an idea that should be seriously considered.

Paul Take the long term view. What would you do with ten grand? By the time you've bought some clothes, got pissed, had a holiday——

Sherry Twenty-three thousand? I haven't got twenty-three pence.

Paul The gap between the haves and the have-nots is increasing all the time. This may be the only chance you ever have to stop being a have-not. I'll get my accountant to beef up your earnings so you look good on paper. Then, all you'd have to do to pay the mortgage would be—to get more successful—or . . .

Sherry Or what?

Paul Nothing.

Sherry Or get a proper job.

Paul Or get a proper job. Nobody here is a chicken any more. That's for certain.

Sherry storms out

(*Shouting*) Will you give the idea some thought?

Paul pauses, then he sits, muttering, and pours a drink

Sherry enters

Sherry You know what this means don't you?

Paul What?

Sherry I would have to stay in my damp room.

Paul Ah.

Sherry All my clothes are getting damp.

Paul Well. That's because the flat belongs to the landlord. Once it belongs to us, we'll have a motive for improving it. Priority number one: the dampness in your room.

Sherry Or we could swap rooms.

Paul Or we could swap rooms.

Sherry goes to the door of Paul and Marion's room and looks in

Sherry I've always liked this room.

Paul OK. If you buy a third, we'll swap rooms.

Sherry You want to stay here an awful lot, don't you?

There is a pause

Paul You've got to have something constant in your life. At least I have. Those awful moments when everything changes. Leaving school. Moving house. Putting things in suitcases, I hate that. You have to fight for some kind of continuity. If you don't have the continuity you just—drift, you lose your grip . . .

There is a moment

Marion enters carrying four empty cardboard boxes

Marion I got these from Sainsbury's. I think we should make a start on the pictures tonight. What are you doing Sherry?
Sherry I was just looking at your room. It's really nice, isn't it?

There is a pause

You'll be sorry to leave it.
Marion Yes. (*To Paul*) The pictures in this big one, yes? And the others will do for books.
Paul You're early aren't you?
Marion Jeremy and I are going to a conference in Reading tomorrow. We've got an early start.

The telephone rings in the hall

You could pack your old records, Sherry, you never play them any more.

Marion exits to answer the telephone

Paul She doesn't mean it.
Sherry You don't have to make excuses for her.
Paul She just thinks it's the best way——
Sherry It freaks me out, you know. You've been going out with her for a whole decade.
Paul It freaks *you* out.
Sherry It can't just be babies. Can it?
Paul Well. I suppose it's never one thing.
Sherry No. I suppose not. I'm really sorry. Is it all right for me to say that?
Paul Yes. It's all right.

Marion enters

Marion (*to Paul*) It's Anthony, he wants to speak to you.
Paul You mean Scott?
Marion Yes.
Paul Why does it always have to be me?

Paul exits to answer the telephone in bad humour

Marion (*looking at the pictures*) I can't remember who these belong to. (*She takes one off the wall and examines it*)
Sherry Are you and Paul getting on OK?
Marion Famously. I suppose this is bound to be his.
Sherry All this uncertainty. The flat and the money and so on. I just feel there's an awful lot of stress around.
Marion I think everyone's coping very well.

There is a pause

Sherry Well. I actually don't think that. I tend to think more the opposite. I think we're all going crazy. And we're going crazy for a basic biological reason. We're animals. Animals need a place to live. Take that away or put it under threat, and they—that is we—begin to behave in all sorts of crazy ways. Have you tried talking to Howard lately? Unless you've got any small talk on the shift from a labour intensive to a capital intensive economy he doesn't want to know. Me? I'm not well, I'm really not. I couldn't even face doing my spot at the *Queen's Head* last Sunday. They had to pull me out at the last minute. I don't know if I can face it this week either. And you—used to be my best friend, and now you don't even tell me you're splitting up with Paul.

There is a pause. Sherry sits down, almost in tears

Marion It's a mistake I suppose, really. You should either get married or split up. This going out together for years and years. I think we rather missed one another at some point. He was always so concerned that marriage and commitment meant losing your personal liberty, I got used to the idea. But I don't think I ever took it that seriously. I mean I assumed secretly that one day he'd stop mucking around and say "OK, this is it for life." But he didn't and I'm now short of time. So it had to end. But—there are financial considerations. There's this wonderful development, Battersea, just what I want. But I need that extra five thousand see? And I shall get it.

Sherry Paul just suggested I should buy this flat with him and Howard.

Marion It would be sensible. You really ought to think of buying somewhere.

Sherry I wouldn't mind doing a bit of travelling actually. I think I'd rather do that.

Paul enters in a state of anxiety

Paul I was called names on that phone.
Marion What did he say?
Paul I was referred to in very unflattering terms.
Marion Is he upset?
Paul Upset? No, he's not *upset*. Upset is what you get when you cut yourself shaving. This man is *murderous*.
Marion Poor darling.
Paul I was called an obstructive fucker on that phone. "You," he said "Are an obstructive fucker. Not only are you screwing me about. You are actively and deliberately getting in my way. And on the basis of this evidence, I do not hesitate to call you an obstructive fucker."
Marion Paul, what did he actually say?
Paul That *is* what he actually——
Marion Did he come up with a new offer?
Paul Yes.

There is a pause

He said it was his absolutely final offer. He said if we didn't accept it, he would personally guarantee that we wouldn't make, and I quote, a brass centime out of the deal. And he means it.
Marion So what's the offer.

There is a pause

Paul There are actually two offers on the table. If we do not accept one of these in the next forty-eight hours, then we can consider ourselves at war with Anthony Scott and his attendant powers of darkness. Offer one: forty-five grand for vacant possession. This works out at eleven thousand two hundred and fifty each.

Marion Shit. (*She sits down suddenly*)

Paul Offer two: he will sell us, all four of us or any combination permed from the four of us, this flat, market value estimated at ninety-five grand, for forty-eight thousand pounds, i.e. he's giving us forty-seven grand. So ... That's it. Any takers?

There is a pause

Marion Sherry?

Sherry OK. I just want to say this. (*Pause*) You asked me to think about buying a share. Well I've thought about it for a full five minutes, and it was misery. I'm a thousand overdrawn in the bank. I'm over the limit on my Access card, my Barclaycard. And I owe people money. I owe all of you money. And on top of that you want me to buy a flat. And yes, I *do* know the phone bill's due again and most of it's mine, and if we could just take the money, I could pay it all, everything, easily, right?

Sherry rushes out

There is a pause

Paul I didn't know she had any credit cards, they must be out of their minds.

Marion Yes.

Marion is thinking rapidly

Paul So. She wants to go. You want to go. So we have to take the money. Unless Howard and I buy the flat. Which would be forty-eight thousand, plus we'd have to buy the two of you off at—twenty-two and a half—which means (*shocked*) seventy thousand plus. We'd have to find thirty-four thousand each, it just can't be—it just can't be done.

Pause

Marion gets up and goes to the picture she's just taken down

Marion We'll do it.

Paul What?

Marion You've discussed the buying option with Howard, yes?

Paul Yes.

Marion Behind my back.

Paul Well tentatively, you know.

Marion I don't mind, it's a good idea.

Paul But Sherry won't——

Marion Howard will though, yes?

Paul What?

Marion Howard is theoretically in?

Paul Well he can raise a reasonable mortgage on his——
Marion So we'll buy it then.

There is a pause

Paul We?
Marion You, me, Howard. We buy the flat for forty-eight, pay Sherry off for eleven two-fifty, call it sixty grand between the three of us. Easy peasy.
Paul Does this mean?
Marion No, it doesn't mean. It's going to be an investment. You can move into Sherry's room. We'll renovate it first.
Paul Renovate.
Marion The whole place. Starting with Sherry's room—*your* room. It'll be nice.
Paul But——
Marion I'll put some money separately into a building fund. I've got a big cash bonus coming from Jeremy. We'll keep accounts and reckon up when we sell the place. All right?
Paul When did you work this out?
Marion Just now.

Marion puts the picture back on the wall

There. We're staying. It's what you wanted, isn't it?

Marion exits

(*Off*) Sherry!

Quick Black-out

Music: "Money for Nothing" by Dire Straits

SCENE 4

The same. October, 1985. A Saturday morning, around eleven o'clock

The room is a little emptier—all the cardboard boxes have gone

Howard is working at the table, attacking the typewriter with vigour

Sherry enters. She is wearing a long white nightdress and drinking a mug of coffee. She stands watching Howard for a few moments

Sherry I've got such a lot to do.

Howard continues to type, muttering to himself

I can't believe I'm really going.

Howard continues to type, muttering to himself

Have they gone out?
Howard Down the building society.

Sherry Oh already?
Howard It shuts at twelve.
Sherry For my money?

Howard writes some more

Great. (*She sips at her coffee*) I'll never get it done.

Howard types some more, then takes the page out of the typewriter and scans it

Howard I don't think anybody else has noticed this.
Sherry What?
Howard Well—historically, for hundreds of years, the British were self-sufficient in food. I mean, we ate what we grew. What happened with the industrial revolution changed all that. We swapped our pre-eminent position as an agricultural nation for dominance as a manufacturing nation, i.e. other nations grew our food for us and we paid for them with ready-made goods. But now, it's changing again. For the first time in history, we are running a deficit on our manufacturing industries. So. Where is our wealth coming from?
Sherry From the building society.
Howard Exactly! That is exactly the right answer!
Sherry Oh.
Howard You are a paradigm of the British economy. You consume more than you produce. You are heavily in debt. But you have managed to keep yourself afloat by selling off your personal share of the national infrastructure—in your case, the right to dwell in a small damp room. Clever isn't it? You stop making new things, instead you tell the world that the things you've already made, the things your grandparents and great-grandparents made, are worth immeasurably more than they were originally. You tell the world over and over again until they start—literally—buying it.
Sherry I've always wanted to be a paradigm.
Howard But there's one problem.
Sherry I thought there might be.
Howard How long will it last? Once the world's evaluation of our infra-structure falls—so do we.
Sherry Christ.
Howard And so do you.

There is a ring at the doorbell

Sherry My money!

Sherry rushes off to answer it

Howard watches her doubtfully. He looks at what he's written. Screws the paper up and throws it on the floor. He inserts a fresh sheet. He pauses a moment, then begins writing again

Sherry enters showing signals of distress

Anthony Scott enters behind her

Howard Oh.

Scott Ah.

Sherry It's—Mr Scott.

Howard Yes.

Scott Is the other chap not in, Paul?

Howard Paul. No he's not, he's—out.

Sherry That's right, and so's Marion.

Howard But they'll be back.

Sherry Yes they've just gone——

Scott Small problem. Nothing earth-shattering. Got a prospective buyer. Ground floor flat. She's upstairs at the moment, having a bit of a prowl.

Howard Oh.

Scott I think she's serious. I should say she's a very serious buyer indeed. This is her second visit, she's got a bloody great laundry list of questions. One of them is about the garden. (*He goes over to the window and stares out*) Such as it is.

Pause

You have access, she has access. The point is. Where does your bit stop and her bit start. Any views? (*He turns towards Sherry and Howard*)

Sherry and Howard are anxious not to commit themselves to a point of view which may later be interpreted as a tactical error by Paul or Marion. So both look blank

Difficult to get a view round here, I tend to find. Everyone has to go into a huddle for a fortnight before coming to a decision. How was it divided up before?

Howard We have use of it. So do the upstairs flat.

Scott But it's on two levels. A smallish bit down on your level. And a biggish bit up on her level.

Howard Yes, but the precedent is both flats use the whole garden.

Scott Well we can't have that. It's not a bloody safari park. It's a piece of property. It needs dividing up. Can I bring her down. Talk about it?

Howard Yes, I don't see why not——

Sherry I must get dressed. (*But she makes no move*)

Scott (*looking at his watch*) Look, I'll nip upstairs. Few points to go through with her. Then I'll bring her down. Paul will be back, you say?

Howard Very soon.

Sherry Very, very soon.

Scott OK then. A few mins. You have been forewarned.

Scott exits

Sherry flaps around, wondering whether to see him out or not. Eventually she decides to

Sherry exits

There is a pause. Howard stares out at the garden looking annoyed

Sherry enters

Howard Just when you think you've—suddenly something else . . .
Sherry What are you saying, Howard?
Howard I want to be left in peace!

There is a pause. Sherry is impressed by this sudden outburst

I'm sorry. I don't mean you. I just mean there are so many hassles. All the legal stuff, getting the mortgage organized. Haggling with Scott. Fine, OK I can live with it for a few months. But it doesn't seem to stop. I mean, I'm trying to write a book about the British Economy. It's a brilliant book, I know it is. But every time I try to get it out of my brain and on to the paper, someone comes barging in telling me to—draw a line down the middle of the garden or something . . .

Sherry goes to him and cuddles him

What I used to like about this flat was the people. I could have gone and bought a little broom cupboard in Neasden years ago. But I didn't because I liked it here. And now you're going. And Marion and Paul are splitting up. And all that's left is the flat. It's hard to work here any more. It's hard to find people to chat to. It's just a building, that's all. An investment.
Sherry You ought to find yourself a nice girl.

Suddenly Paul and Marion burst in, excitedly

Marion holds a large brown envelope. Paul carries a tray on which are four glasses and a bottle of champagne

Marion Oh look, a moving human scene.
Paul For Christ's sake, you two. You've been living in adjacent rooms for a decade, don't start getting it together now she's leaving.
Sherry We were just having an innocent, sentimental——
Paul Champagne time. We thought this event should not go uncelebrated. (*He starts peeling off the top of the bottle*)
Marion (*brandishing the envelope*) It's all here. Exactly as you wanted it.

Sherry catches Marion and Paul's excitement

Sherry Quick, quick, let me see it.
Marion No, you have to wait a moment.
Paul For the champagne, these things have to be done properly.
Marion Where's your key?
Sherry My key?
Marion Door key.
Sherry Oh.

Sherry exits

Paul (*to Howard*) Hold a glass so I don't spill any.
Howard I think we're going to have a problem with the garden——
Paul Not *now*——
Marion We want to give Sherry a nice send off——

Paul Not that she's going to get off the premises by midnight at the current rate of progress——

Marion If she's not out by midnight, we could start charging her rent.

Paul laughs

> *Sherry enters holding a Yale key*

Paul Right, here we go.

Paul opens the champagne and pours it into the glasses

Howard distributes the glasses

Sherry Who's paying for this?

Marion What?

Sherry The champagne? Is it coming out of my money?

Marion The syndicate is paying. Paul, Howard and me. We have just bought ourselves a slice of London.

Sherry Let me look at it, let me see the——

Paul Not yet! (*He looks around*) Everyone has a glass? Yes. Now then. (*Mock formal address*) Dearly beloved brethren. We are gathered here today to mark the demise from these rented premises of our dear sister, Sherry St George, née Martin. History will ask but one question: Did she fall or was she pushed? I think the answer will come ringing back loud and clear "A bit of both". God bless her and all who sail in her!

All drink, offering various toasts

> Now if you'd like to step forward.

Sherry steps forward

Marion In exchange for your front door key, I hereby present you with a cheque for ten thousand pounds.

Sherry examines the cheque carefully

> · And an envelope full of twenty pound notes to the sum of one thousand, two hundred and fifty pounds

Howard They can't all be twenties——

Paul Sixty-two twenties and one ten.

Sherry takes the cheque and the envelope. Marion takes the key

Marion It felt terrible walking down the street with it all——

Sherry I don't think I've ever seen so much money before and it's all mine.

Howard Paul, there's something important——

Paul Wait a minute——

Sherry opens the envelope. She lets the money fall out all over the floor, kneels down and runs her hands through it

Sherry It's so lovely. It really is so beautiful.

· *There is a moment, while Marion, Paul and Howard watch Sherry with the money*

Then Sherry lets out a whoop

Sherry hugs Marion, then Paul

> (*She is quite tearful*) Thank you. Thank you.

Sherry swigs some champagne down and gives Howard a half-hug

> I'm sorry I was a bit of a pain. I was so afraid we'd end up with nothing. You were great, all of you being so strong. (*A thought strikes her*) Oh. I owe you all some of this. Paul.

Sherry hands Paul a twenty pound note

Paul Oh. Are you sure this is——
Sherry Marion.

Sherry hands Marion a twenty pound note

Sherry Howard.

Sherry hands Howard three twenty pound notes

Howard is embarrassed, not wanting the others to know how much he's lent her

Marion This is too much, you only owe me——
Sherry No, it's not too much. It's too little, I know there's lots of things I haven't paid for over the years.
Marion Sherry——
Sherry No, I won't hear a word of it. It's not too much, it isn't nearly enough. This champagne is heaven. (*She gulps some more down*)

Paul tops up her glass

Sherry delves deeper into the pile of money

Paul You're welcome.
Sherry No, I've decided, you're all to have some more. There's all sorts of things I've used over the years.
Paul Sherry, just steady, all right——
Sherry Washing-up liquid, soap, all sorts of things. (*She picks up three more twenty pound notes*)
Marion Please. Sherry, put it all back in the envelope.
Sherry *Toilet rolls!* Do you know the last time I bought a toilet roll? Have another one of these. (*She proffers three more twenty pound notes*)
Paul It's all OK. It's all absolutely——
Sherry Nineteen seventy-nine, that's when! In Dieppe. It was Bastille Day and I had chronic diarrhoea——
Marion You don't owe any of us anything——
Sherry Streaming! And I went into this whatsit—Monoprix and bought a roll and I thought Christ, I had no idea it was so expensive——

There is a ring at the bell

Howard Christ!

Sherry gets to her feet and tries to force money on everyone

It's Scott. He's got this woman upstairs.
Paul Really?
Howard A buyer. It's about the garden, we've got to divide it up.
Marion I don't get this.
Howard Marion, just sort her out.

Howard drags Paul with him to the hall, explaining all the way

She's buying the ground floor flat. But she wants to know how much of
the garden is hers and how much is . . .

Howard and Paul exit

Sherry is getting more tearful. She swigs some champagne

Marion What's all this about Scott?

Sherry drinks some more

Sherry I'm going to miss you all so much. It's been such a long time. I only
wish there'd been some way. If only we could have found a way. For me
to stay, it would have been . . .

Marion peers down the corridor

Marion (*realizing that Scott is the impending visitor*) Listen, we must clear
up all this money—
Sherry No, it's mine, leave it alone.
Marion Sherry, it's Scott, he's coming up the corridor now——
Sherry I like it. I like feeling it.

Sherry pushes Marion away

Leave it.

Marion freezes, unable to make up her mind what to do

I wish I didn't have to go. (*She reaches for the champagne bottle*) I really
wish that.

Paul enters, followed by Scott. Howard enters bringing up the rear

*Paul, Scott and Howard pause in the doorway, transfixed by the sight of
Sherry, who is kneeling in a pile of twenty pound notes in her nightie, with tears
streaming down her face, clutching the champagne bottle*

They're throwing me out!
Scott Well they're having more success than I ever did.
Marion It's all right, she's just a little——
Scott Now, I mentioned when I was down earlier——
Howard Yes, well they've only just come in, so I've not had time to——
Sherry There's a woman in the garden staring at me. (*In the direction of the
garden*) Fuck off!
Scott Ah yes, that's the prospective buyer. Claire Kinross, the Honourable
Claire Kinross.
Howard Oh Christ.

Sherry starts to struggle up on a chair so she can abuse Claire through the top of the window

Sherry That's our garden you know, you can't just wander round it like it was Brent Cross shopping centre——
Scott (*to Paul*) Yes well, the thing is, the garden.
Sherry They hate me! They've always hated me. And now they're buying me off. That's how you really show you hate someone. By giving them piles of money. It's the biggest fucking insult in the world.

There is a pause. Paul, Marion, Scott and Howard stare at Sherry

Paul The best way, actually, into the garden is through this door here. (*He makes for his and Marion's bedroom door*)

Paul exits through the door. Scott exits after him

Howard (*flapping*) Do something with her.

Howard exits

Marion (*staring at Sherry*) Sherry will you please sit on that chair, please.

Sherry immediately goes to sit at the table, among Howard's papers

Give me the bottle.

Sherry gives Marion the bottle. Marion puts it on the mantelpiece, then starts clearing up the money into the brown envelope

Sherry (*watching her*) There's something so ... admirable about you. There always has been. You are so contained. People look at you, they admire you. You should have done better for yourself, you've got so much ... class, so much cool. I've sat and admired your cool for hours at a stretch. At University there were all these dozens of men. Following you around. They used to plan their day around the possibility of catching a glimpse of your cool. Money would change hands for library seats affording a good view of you. It wasn't lust, it was fascination with the outer limits of cool. I loved being your best friend. But I always wanted you to say it. I wanted you to say "Sherry, you're my best friend." But I knew you wouldn't. If you'd said that, it wouldn't have been cool.

Marion has all the money in the envelope

Marion (*looking at Sherry*) Sherry ... (*Pause*) I think it would be a good idea if you took this money into your room and got dressed.
Sherry Yes. I've got such a lot to do. I've got to pack all the rest of my things and clear out of my room. And write all those cheques. Phone calls, must phone my mum. Load all my stuff on to the van by three o'clock for Paul to drive to my auntie's. Pick up my travellers' cheques and currency from American Express, get to the airport by ... When do I have to be at the——
Marion Nine o'clock——
Sherry Nine o'clock, right. And I shall get on the plane and drink lots and fall asleep watching the film. Then wake up in San Francisco.

Marion Yes. You're glad you're going, aren't you?

Sherry I'm going to love it, I'm going to absolutely adore it. I used to say, when I was a little girl "I'm going to go round the world." And now I really am.

Marion Yes. Please get dressed, or you'll be behind schedule.

Sherry stands

Sherry I'm sorry about just now. It was handing in my key that did it. It suddenly hit me that I was leaving.

Marion (*looking out of the window*) I think they're going to come back in.

Sherry I must ... I don't want them to see me.

Marion Just put some old jeans on, for the packing. I'll come and help you in a minute.

Sherry Yes. (*She heads for the door*)

Marion (*brandishing the envelope*) Sherry. Take your money.

Sherry (*taking the envelope*) Oh yes.

Marion Put it under your pillow for now, right?

Sherry Pillow. Right. Yes.

Sherry exits

Marion looks out at the garden. Then she does some hasty tidying up. She quickly adjusts her own appearance

Scott, Paul and Howard enter

Marion Is it all right?

Scott I've suggested a dividing line. When you've talked it over, you can telephone my lawyers. (*He smiles. To Paul*) So. Quick decision on this one, please. If need be, make a drawing and bike it round to me. Then we'll be ready to exchange on Wednesday, all right?

Paul Yes, fine.

Scott (*looking around*) Big flat. You got it bloody cheap. One of these, identical, just round the corner, went the other day for a hundred. So you're well in.

Paul Well, we're quite pleased.

Scott I should say. (*He makes to go, then turns for a moment*) Oh just one last thing. (*Pleasantly*) You're bastards. You're a bunch of grasping, capitalist bastards. Congratulations. Wasn't too difficult, was it?

Scott exits

Howard sits and looks at his notes

Howard It's not real wealth, that's the point. There's no substance to it.

Sherry enters. She is still in her nightie

Sherry Marion. Did I take that money or did I leave it here?

Marion You put it under your pillow.

Sherry Pillow, of course. (*She goes to the champagne bottle, and drinks from it*) I've got such a lot to do.

Quick Black-out

ACT II

Scene 1

The same. May 1986. Early afternoon. A hot day

Music: "You Can Call Me Al" by Paul Simon

The room is now completely bare. The carpet has been taken up and every single object removed. A huge dust cloth covers the floor

For several moments nothing happens at all. Then for the first time in the play, the French windows open. In fact, they fly open at the combined push of Paul and Howard who come in from the garden carrying between them a large plastic dustbin full of rubble

Paul is wearing only a pair of cut-off jeans. Howard a tee-shirt and a pair of old trousers. Both look tired and dirty. After a few stumbling paces towards the corridor with the dustbin of rubble, it becomes clear that Howard can't carry it any further. They come to a halt in the middle of the room

Howard No, no, no, just leave——
Paul Don't, not like that——
Howard Down! Put it——
Paul For fuck's sake!

They stop and breathe heavily

You can't just——
Howard Yes, I know——
Paul Well, if you know then——
Howard Yes, yes, all right yes.

They breathe heavily again

Silly bastard.
Paul What?
Howard Him, not you. He's filled it too full. Silly bastard.

There is a pause

Paul goes to the French windows

Paul (*calling*) Stewart! You are the subject of some criticism here.

Howard is sitting on the floor, completely exhausted

A section of the workforce is refusing to co-operate with the new norms.

Paul turns back to Howard, surveying him

Stewart enters. He is around forty, strong, bearded. He wears old jeans, no shirt and carries a pickaxe. He stands in the doorway, looking at Howard

Stewart What's up?

Howard There's too much rubble in the dustbin.

Stewart Too much? How can there be too much?

Howard (*looking at Stewart; suddenly animated*) You chip it out with the pickaxe, right? And shovel it in the bin, right? And we walk it down the corridor and through to the skip, right? But if you put too much in the bin, we can't carry it. It doesn't get to the skip. It stays here in the middle of the floor.

Stewart I thought you were supposed to be working-class, Howard.

Howard I am not *supposed* to be working-class, I *am* working-class.

Stewart The whole point of the working-class is that they should be able to work.

Howard It is *too heavy!!*

Stewart puts the pick down

Stewart Paul?

Stewart motions Paul to the bin. They pick it up with relative ease

Stewart and Paul exit out of the door with the bin

Howard sits defeated

Howard (*at the end of his tether and trying not to cry*) I just ... want it ... to stop ... (*He reaches into his pocket for a cigarette. He lights it, and smokes it, trying to pull himself together*)

There is a pause

Marion enters. She is very smartly dressed. She carries a Next bag which obviously contains an exciting new clothes' purchase

Marion Hello. (*She goes to the French windows and looks out*) You boys. You do have your fun and games. (*She turns and looks at Howard*) Is Paul annoyed with me?

Howard What?

Marion He just passed me in the corridor without saying hello.

Howard Was he carrying two and a half hundredweight of shite at the time?

Marion Yes.

Howard I wouldn't take it personally then.

There is a pause

Marion Are you all right?

Howard No.

There is a pause

I don't think I can take it any more. Let's do the flat up ourselves, let's save money. OK, I'll do that, I'm on the bus. Why pay a load of cowboys ten grand to excavate our half of the garden when we can do it ourselves for five hundred quid? These guys, they're not clever, they're not especially skilled, all you're paying for is hard physical labour.

There is a pause

Well personally, I think they deserve it, all that money. I think hard physical labour *should* carry high rewards. I tell you one thing, I remember now why I stuck at my books when I was a lad. Anything to avoid looking like me dad did after a double shift at the shipyard. I worked one day there, Christmas Vac, nineteen seventy-one. Couldn't stand up the next day. Physically, could not stand up, get out of bed, anything. That's how I got my first. Fear of hard physical labour. And now here I am, doing this. I'm not practical enough to be the foreman, and I'm not fit enough to do the donkey work. This, this is what I've been trying to get away from all my life. I just want to be in a quiet room, surrounded by books, writing. Yesterday I took the top off a bottle of Tippex to remind me of the smell. It was beautiful.

There is a pause

Howard is moved

Marion is embarrassed by this confidence. She makes a move to touch him, then changes her mind

> *Stewart enters, carrying the empty bin*

Stewart Sorry about that Howard, you were right. I scraped my shin dragging the bugger up the steps. (*He claps Howard matily round the shoulder*) Must not get carried away. Must not get carried away.

Stewart exits, taking the bin out into the garden

Paul enters, carrying a postcard

Paul Second post. (*To Marion, mock surprise*) Oh hello. Guess who it's from.
Marion It isn't! (*She snatches the postcard*)
Paul It is.
Marion From Sherry, wonderful, Paraguay!
Paul Well yes, the picture on the front is Paraguay.
Howard (*looking over Marion's shoulder*) But the postmark is Senegal.
Marion Oh yes. (*Reading*) "Here I am in Burundi."

> *Stewart enters. He stands in the doorway*

"The most amazing things keep happening to me. Everywhere there is poverty, but mingled with the picturesque. It all seems a long time ago, the flat and everything. Money lasts longer here and it is truly a better existence. But I'll be back in the autumn. Love to you all, Sherry." Well.
Stewart So now you know. They live better over there.
Paul In Burundi.
Howard Or Senegal or Paraguay.
Marion It's not exactly ...

Howard Packed with those clinching details which are the hallmark of the great foreign correspondent.
Marion Quite.
Stewart Synchronicity, this is the thing.

Marion, Paul and Howard look at him blankly

Synchronicity. A child is dying in Burundi. Say it's three o'clock in the afternoon. At exactly the same moment, an armed mob storms the gates of the President's palace in Paraguay and a couple in Senegal are screwing in blissful delirium on the damp earth of the rain forest. All these events are connected. A shift in a molecule here, a nudge of an atom there, and the child is dead, the dictator on the scrap heap of history and the couple totally shagged out and wondering what to do for the rest of the afternoon. It's like working in your garden. I swing the pickaxe and a shudder runs through the earth's core. Somewhere in Papua New Guinea, a child is born.

Stewart goes back into the garden

Marion Is he all right?
Paul He used to be a DJ on Radio Caroline in the Sixties.
Howard Although I don't think the current situation in Paraguay is nearly as dynamic as he suggested. I mean is it really possible that——

Howard realizes he is boring them and exits into the garden

Paul and Marion look at each other. There is a pause

Marion Hello.
Paul Been out?
Marion Yes.
Paul Long time.
Marion Not really, I just got in very late last night and had to get into the office early this morning.
Paul On a Saturday?
Marion Got the new launch coming up in ten days time. It isn't a doss there any more. I had to proof-read the leaflets.
Paul Funny, we got up at half-six. Didn't hear you.
Marion Quiet as a mouse, me.

She stares him out, daring him to disbelieve it

Paul I went into your room. You weren't there. You weren't there at midnight. Or seven in the morning, or at any time in between. I know you were with Jeremy.
Marion All right, I was with Jeremy.
Paul We're not meant to be a couple any more. You don't have to buy a dress from Next on the way back to make me think you've been out shopping.
Marion If we're not meant to be a couple, how come you're going into my room at all hours checking up?

There is a pause. They both sit

It's not working. We're still living together so it feels as if we're still ...
together. But we're not. Everything's changed and yet ... everything still
goes on the same.

Paul Well I'm sorry, but we decided on a course of action and we can't
change our minds now.

Marion I'm not talking about changing our minds, I'm talking about my
feelings——

Paul Feelings don't come into it. We bought the flat together and while
we're halfway through the building work we won't be able to sell it. And
of course, since we can't afford to pay the ludicrous prices charged by so-
called professional builders, we have to do it ourselves. So it's slow, very
slow, but there it is. We've just got to lump it.

Marion I hate the whole fucking business. Separate bedrooms. It takes me
an hour to fall asleep every night. At least an hour. I don't know what
your life is like any more. After all those years. I don't know what you're
doing, where you go. I get jealous, with or without cause I don't know,
I've no idea if you get jealous——

Paul Of course I get jealous, why d'you think I check up on you. I'd guessed
about Jeremy, you knew I'd guessed.

Marion Talk about being out of practice. I had been so monumentally
faithful to you. It took me three months to realize that he wasn't just
impressed by my new found industry. In the old days, when I was just
mooching round the office clocking up the minimum, he wasn't interested. As soon as I started putting in every waking hour, I would catch
him staring at my legs. Same legs. Only industry is sexy to Jeremy.
Adrenalin, power, all that go-for-it mentality. We're making so much
money, you wouldn't believe. Just a little hole in the corner operation a
few years back, then suddenly, wammo, you identify a gap in the market,
you square up the state of the art technology with consumer demand and
then you work and work and work till you're there. Our service, what we
provide is actually brilliant, no hype, no bullshit. And to be absolutely
honest, I love it, I adore it. It's only when I stop ... come back here ...
stare at the Bob Dylan poster on the loo door ...

*Howard and Stewart enter and stagger through with another bin of rubble.
They macho this up as much as possible. They go off*

Paul So what do you want to do?

Marion Well. I don't see it would be a disadvantage to sell in the current
state. You need three things—location, quantity and quality. Well we've
got the first two. The quality is something a buyer could work on. The
potential's here, that's the important thing.

Paul You want to move in with Jeremy. That's what you're saying——

Marion I'm not saying that. I don't know. Maybe. All I'm saying is I can't
stand *this*. I could get a place on my own, you and Howard could chip in
together. Everyone would be happy. Or at least, no-one would be
downright bloody miserable.

Paul I have to see this through. The building. It's the one thing I've
concentrated on to keep me sane. I can't just throw it over now. After the
garden, we're doing the damp in my room. Comes from that old sink.
Take the sink out, dig up the rotten floorboards, burn them. Then dig
down, improve the circulation of air underneath, replace the joists and the
boards and there you are. Stewart's got a mate who deals in pine, we can
do the whole job for a hundred quid. It's satisfying me, don't you see that?

Marion And the music biz?

Paul That piece on the new Paul Simon album. *Q Magazine* want an
expanded version.

Marion Thank Christ for Paul Simon. You'd be sunk if you had to write
about someone new, eh?

Stewart enters

Stewart You know those four pieces of timber we need for the supports?

Paul The three be two?

Stewart The three be two. Well, we only need three of them now.

*Howard enters. He carries an estate agent's "For Sale" sign mounted on a
seven foot length of three by two*

Howard Seven foot of three be two.

Stewart It suddenly fell away from the property it was advertising.

Howard Straight into our honest hands.

Stewart This is my point about synchronicity, you see. You need a piece of
wood, you don't go out and buy it. You wait for *it* to come to *you*.

Marion Is that ... I mean isn't that theft?

Howard From estate agents? No, no, you see, if all property is theft, then
who is more culpable?

Stewart exits into the garden, leaving the estate agent's sign on the floor

It's quite a profound idea really. The advertisement for the property
actually becomes *part* of the property.

Howard follows Stewart out

(*Off*) A case of the sign as signifier becoming the signified.

Paul See, Howie's cheered up already, it doesn't take much does it?

Marion Is that a warning to make me buck up?

Paul It would help. The morale of the troops.

Marion You find out I've been screwing my boss and all you're worried
about is the morale of the troops. You can't summon a full committee
meeting of flat members to deal with this problem.

Stewart enters

Stewart She's making peculiar noises.

Paul I'm sorry.

Stewart That very rich, very titled lady who has purchased the flat above
yours. She's making noises which indicate displeasure about our
excavations.

Paul Oh give me a break.

Stewart I think maybe a personal intervention——

Paul is already on his way out to the garden

(*Taking the opportunity to rest*) They are doing very well, those boys. Do you know, they've transported nearly two tons of London clay down that corridor by purely manual means. If my calculations are correct, this is the equivalent of carrying an average-sized man from here to Surbiton and back. (*Thinking*) Yes Surbiton. And they have learned a fundamental truth about life, namely that the whole of the building trade is one enormous rip-off. No special skills are required. You've just got to be prepared to get your hands dirty. Any human being of moderate intelligence can build a home from scratch. I've built two myself, one in County Cork, one in Brittany. They're still standing. It's a primitive urge, the yearning to place one stone on top of another. But you make an awful lot more money out of it than you do flogging away at the old nine to five.

Marion What does she want?

Stewart The rich bitch?

Marion Claire.

Stewart A territorial dispute. You can't blame her. With land at a hundred quid per square foot. I'd be jumpy if someone started tunnelling in my backyard.

Marion Do you enjoy all this?

Stewart The labouring game? There's a certain satisfaction yes.

Marion What sort of satisfaction?

Stewart My woman just walked out on me. It's a natural cycle. A woman walks out on me, I do some building work to take my mind off it. Eventually I end with a new house or a renovated flat. There you are, a single man living in semi-palatial circumstances. For some reason, this combination of factors is sensationally attractive to women. Before you know where you are, a woman has moved in. Things go very well, then less well, then rather badly. Eventually she walks out and to stop being depressed you sell up, buy a ruin and start to renovate it. Then, before you know where you are, etcetera. That's why I'm working here. Doing up someone else's place means I won't be tempted to lure a woman back to the luxury pad which will eventually emerge from the ruins. In this way I will be delivered from the cycle and will be able to do something sensible with my life. You've done well out of this place, what did you buy it for?

Marion Forty-eight.

Stewart Be worth a hundred and twenty now, more when we've built the patio.

Paul enters, angry. Howard follows him

Paul The nerve of these people. Her family own half of Cornwall and she starts belly-aching about two square foot of London clay.

Stewart What's the problem?

Paul There is now no problem. I sorted her out. She says "We agreed the dividing line between your property and mine should be three point five metres away from the back wall. Why are you excavating to a line four point five metres from the back wall."

Marion Doesn't she have a point?

Paul I had to spell it out to her "We are building a retaining wall. What will it be retaining? Several tons of earth. In order to prevent the weight of the earth pressing directly on to the wall and pushing it over, we have to start digging further back, *then* build the wall, *then* fill in the gap with loose rubble."

Stewart That was telling her.

Paul She went very quiet, I can tell you. Don't they teach them anything at Bedales?

Howard Mind you, we should have asked her permission. To dig on her land you know.

Paul She's never here. Anyway she's getting the benefit of our work. She's getting a free irrigation system. It really pisses me off.

Howard indicates to Stewart that they should get to work

Howard exits into the garden

Stewart The earth. The pitiless earth.

Stewart follows Howard out

Paul This used to be an interesting area. Now it's full of people like her.

Marion Why do you have to talk about her like that?

Paul What?

Marion Claire. I had a chat with her the other day. I like her. You should see what she's doing to her flat. She's got taste.

Paul She's got money.

Marion It's not a sin to be rich. She was *born* rich, she can't help it. At least she has the grace to wear her wealth with a certain degree of style——

Stewart and Howard enter with another bin of rubble

Stewart Did I say Surbiton? I think I meant Winchester.

Stewart and Howard exit

Paul You want to put it on the market, don't you? And move in with Jeremy. Does he want children?

Marion No.

Paul Oh. Doesn't that rather ...

Marion No.

Paul Have you changed your mind?

Marion Did I say I wanted to move in with Jeremy?

Paul No.

Marion Did I say I wanted Jeremy at all?

Paul You said you wanted children.

Marion And no-one ever changes their mind. Everything stays true for ever.

(*She goes towards her bedroom door and opens it*)

Marion exits, leaving the door open

Paul stares at the open door

(*Off*) Paul.

Paul I ... I have to work.

Marion (*off*) Stewart can cope. It stops him from being unhappy.

Paul stands for a few moments. He hears Stewart and Howard approaching

    Paul exits into Marion's bedroom and shuts the door

There is a pause

    Howard enters. He carries two more estate agent's signs. He flings them on to the floor

Howard Blue collar crime. You get a taste for it.

    Stewart enters with another estate agent's sign and the empty bin

    (*Calling through the french windows*) Paul!

Stewart throws the sign down on the floor

Stewart And there's your four supports. Completely gratis and for nothing. See what I mean. It's the pagan philosophy, what the Anglo-Saxons called "wyrd". Fate. Don't go out searching for what you want. Stay put, send your message out along the web and what you want will come to you. Wyrd. The web of Wyrd.

Black-out

Music: "Don't Leave Me This Way" by The Communards

Scene 2

The same. November, 1986. Early evening

The room is still bare, but there are new curtains and a handsome wooden floor. In the middle of the floor is a newly delivered carpet, large enough to cover about two thirds of the floor. It is wrapped in thick brown paper. To one side is a sleeping bag and a rucksack, an oasis of mess in the cool order

Howard is sitting on the rolled up carpet smoking a cigarette. He wears a heavy overcoat. Next to him is a black holdall

Sherry, in her nightdress, is pacing around

Sherry So we get on the boat at Bilbao, about five thousand of us. Wedged. We're not talking sardines, we're talking mashed tuna. With no edible oil. There's these four nuns, they get so squashed, people start thinking they're newspapers. And in the middle of all this mayhem, I suddenly think "I'm going back. I'm going back, after thirteen months to that funny little island." And just at that point I'm hit by this giant wave of nausea. And I'm nowhere near the side of the boat. And it's too packed to make it to the rail. I reach for a newspaper, it turns out to be a nun. It's a huge crisis, I can't hold it back any longer. I try to smile and think of England. Only the more I think of England, the more I want to be sick. Then suddenly it happens. This Swede. Or maybe he's a Lapp. Or a Finn. One of that lot who have arrows going through their vowels, he comes up to me, these enormous blue eyes, real icy blue, the genuine boring holes through your retina jobs, he comes up to me and says "Do you believe in hypnotism?" At this stage, I'm prepared to believe in anything that'll stop me embossing the nearest habit with last night's dinner, so I say——

Howard Sherry——

Sherry "Of course I believe in hypnotism"—what?

Howard It's so good to see you. Only——

Sherry Yes?

Howard Like I've only just come back from a weekend in Govan which might not seem a very big deal, but——

Sherry Oh God, yes, Marion said——

Howard No, no——

Sherry About your dad, they both told me last night, it's so selfish of me——

Howard It's no big deal.

Sherry Just forgot in the heat of the——

Howard It was three months ago now. It's all right, life goes on, he's better off out of it, it's just my mum. She's got nothing to do all day. I mean, I'm there, what, three days, she's following me round the house all the time like a lost thing. Emptied me ashtray three times during the same fag, I swear it. What can you do? There's only two people left on the estate she knows, she gets lost in the daft shopping centre ...

Sherry I'm really sorry.

Sherry hugs Howard, embarrassing him

Howard Get off! Look, this carpet. Did it just walk in or what?

Sherry Oh no it was delivered. Couple of hours ago. I was dead impressed. Both the guys on the van had Eton accents.

Howard But you're sure it was for here?

Sherry The chit's got Marion's name on it.

Howard Only I didn't know about it. Should be a communal decision spending money.

Sherry Never mind money. Tell me about you. Your love life.

Howard Usual, you know, who's got the time?

Sherry Well, almost everybody in my experience.

Howard I've been working on the book. That and all the bastard DIY. Keeps you busy. Resigned all me NATFHE commitments, Labour Party never sees me.

Sherry It's not good for you.

Howard It's the deal though, eh. When the time comes to look after number one, there's not a lot of room for anything else in your life.

Sherry Did you really do this floor, it's wonderful.

Howard Well I helped, like. Paul and his mate Stewart, they were the gaffers. Paul's got very canny at it. And dead particular too, finicky you know.

Sherry The patio looks brilliant.

Howard Nearly killed me. And I'm dreading the kitchen. Paul's been making drawings, studying the plumbing, visiting building centres. We'll be months at it.

Sherry He seems happy.

Howard Yeah. Only . . . (*Pause*) He doesn't spend any time on his work. Doesn't seem interested. Knocks off the articles and interviews in a few minutes, then spends a whole day fiddling around with a bit of wiring. Reckons it's a better way of making money. Never has any cash these days.

There is the sound of the front door shutting

Sherry It's lovely to see you. Paul and Marion are they . . . ?

Howard What?

Sherry Well, sort of . . .

Howard Don't ask me, I only live here. Honestly I couldn't tell you if——

Paul and Marion enter. Marion wears a very expensive coat. Paul carries a small cardboard box

Marion Howard. Was it OK?

Marion kisses Howard lightly on the cheek

Paul claps Howard round the shoulder

Howard Yeah, all right, you know. Got in about four hours ago, haven't got me coat off yet.

Paul Highlights of the world tour, takes a while.

Sherry Wait till I get the slides.

Marion Oh it's arrived.

They all look at the carpet

Paul What is it?

Marion Well what does it look like?

Paul I didn't think we'd made any decisions about—

Marion Have you got a knife?

Paul reaches in his pocket and produces a complex Swiss Army knife

When you see this, you'll be completely stunned.

Howard When you look at the quality of their weaponry, it's amazing the Swiss Army don't have a better historical record.

Paul has started cutting through the cords. Everyone gathers around to nudge and coax the carpet into position

Marion Sherry, I think your things are going to be slightly in the way.

Sherry Oh yes, sorry. I'll . . . (*She pushes her sleeping bag and travel effects against the wall*) It's a dead comfortable floor, I slept really well.

Paul Marion, if you stand on the paper, Howard and I will roll it out . . .

Marion Right, got it.

Paul (*to Sherry*) Out the way.

They unroll the carpet. It's sumptuous. All are stunned into silence

Howard Big, isn't it?

Sherry They've got bigger ones in India. Like this, but bigger, I saw them.

Marion I'm so pleased. I think it's exactly right.

Paul Um, look, I didn't think we'd made any decisions about ...

Marion And I think you'll find we can get away with very minimal dressing of the rest of the room. This makes such a simple bold statement. And then a fun thing somewhere—here, to take the edge off the severity. I know. That plant in my room.

Sherry Yes.

Marion I'll get it, see how it looks.

Marion exits

There is silence. Paul sees the delivery docket on the mantelpiece, picks it up, reads it

Paul Howie, remember that carpet warehouse in the Harrow Road we went to.

Howard Oh aye, we brought back some swatches.

Paul D'you think this one's better?

Howard Better? Well of course it's better.

Paul How much better?

Howard (*catching his drift*) How much?

Paul I'm asking you.

Howard Don't piss around. How much did it cost?

Paul Two thousand six hundred and eighty-seven.

Howard Pounds?

Paul Pounds.

There is a pause. Then Howard goes to Paul, and snatches the docket from him and examines it

Howard Two six eight seven. That's the delivery number.

Paul Well why's it got a squiggle with two lines going through it in front of it?

Howard Because it means pounds. I'm an economist, that means pounds. Two thousand six hundred and eighty-seven. For a carpet.

Sherry It's just a big rug really.

Paul Now, tell me how much you like it.

Howard I love it, I want to die on it.

Marion enters with the plant. She stands it in a corner

Marion There. That's the sort of thing.

Paul Erm, we were wondering ...

Marion This is my purchase. You can enjoy the benefits of it. I was very depressed by the swatches you brought back from the Harrow Road. And I was talking to Claire and we went out and bought it. Claire's right, she says money spent on the best is never wasted.

Sherry Well it certainly ... I mean it brings out what you've done with the rest of the room so well.

Marion The other thing is the kitchen. I was thinking perhaps we ought to pay some men to come in and do it. I mean, it's not like the rest of the house. You can't go for months without a kitchen, can you? If I don't have somewhere I can cook, I go crazy. The people who did Claire's are very good, and not unreasonable. Five thousand or something. And it would be done in a fortnight. We could all go away and when we came back it would be done.

Paul But I've ordered the wood for the units. I measured it all up. There's all this wood coming.

Marion Well it's just wood.

Marion exits

Paul (*gesturing to the cardboard box*) I bought this junction box today. I've planned where the lights go. (*To Howard*) Did you know about this?

Howard She's been making muttering noises. About how long it's all been taking. I didn't know she would——

Paul Paying good money. To other people. For things we could do ourselves.

Sherry Well. I suppose she's right in a way. A good kitchen—is a good kitchen, isn't it?

Paul My kitchen would be a good kitchen. What she'll get is some bunch of cowboys sticking in standard units. Quick grown steam-dried pine. Where's the individuality in that? Where's the pride?

Howard Come on Paul. We've flogged ourselves to death on this the last eighteen months. All right, we've saved money, but look what it's cost us. The energy we've spent on it. Which should have gone into other things. Look at my work. Look at *your* work for Christ's sake. There's a stack of unplayed records on your desk you should have reviewed. Records some people would kill for, you get them free and you haven't even broken them out of the cellophane. What's that about, man?

Paul sits down suddenly, says nothing

Sherry This flat. It must be worth quite a bit now, eh?

Howard I suppose.

Sherry I mean, that eleven thousand I took. What would that be worth? If I'd done what you did?

Howard I dunno. It's a bit complex. I mean there's a lot of factors.

Sherry No there aren't. You must have some idea what the flat's worth.

Howard Well it's, I mean if you take——

Paul Twenty-five thousand. If you'd done what we did. Instead of your eleven grand two fifty. Twenty-five thousand pounds.

Sherry Oh.

Marion enters, bringing in a new drinks cabinet. She sets it down

This Scandinavian hypnotist I met on the crossing. He was really nice. he bought me dinner on the boat. And the train fare to London. All I had left was a few pesetas, you see. Seventeen pesetas. That's all I had left out of eleven thousand pounds. I didn't know how I was going to make it back.

So it was great that he turned up. I mean, I slept with him. In his cabin. But it was still nice of him. He was an OK Swede. Finn.

There is a pause

Howard Well yeah, but you've been round the world. Really thoroughly, not just the obvious places. Not many people have done that. Burundi and places. That's worth spending a lot of money on. You can't put a price on that.
Sherry Burundi?
Howard You sent us a card from Burundi.
Sherry Oh yes ... Burundi. Yes, everyone was really nice there.
Howard You did the adventurous thing. We were boring just—staying here.

Sherry stands

Sherry Is it all right if I go and have a bath. I haven't had a bath for an awful long time. (*She grabs some things*)

Sherry exits hurriedly

Howard Christ, Paul. You shouldn't have said that, about the money we've made.
Paul I think I'd like some discussion about this kitchen business.
Marion Well of course.
Paul I want to do the kitchen myself. It's the thing I've been really looking forward to. And I know I can do it well. And I want to be given the chance.
Marion And how long will it take you? Six months? A year?
Paul I don't know!

There is a pause

Marion What do you think, Howard?
Howard Well. Suppose we look at this as a hypothesis, this getting builders in. We've done the patio. We ripped out all the damp in Paul's room. We transformed the bathroom. Put in central heating. Decorated Marion's room, the corridor. Now, if we accept what Marion's putting forward, getting builders in, that's the kitchen done. With the carpet down in here it means ... Well it means we've finished, doesn't it? It actually means we've finished.
Paul What about your room?
Howard It'll do.

There is a pause

It's over Paul. We've done it. We can go back to, you know, normal life.
Paul What about the money? I can't afford five grand. I can't even afford a third of five grand.
Marion I've made arrangements. We account for everything in the accounting book. I pay real money to the builders and get theoretical credits from you two against the time when we come to sell.

Marion goes to Paul and touches him tenderly

Paul, be reasonable, it's got to be like this.

Paul looks at them both

Paul You've set this up between you, haven't you?

Howard What?

Paul Behind my back.

Howard First I've heard of it, man.

Paul I'm going to have to think very carefully about this. I'm going to have to consider my position.

Howard Accept it. It's over. Don't you feel relieved?

Paul Look at what we've done. Look at what I've done. Bought a flat in a Victorian house in a London conservation area for peanuts. At the start of a property boom. And renovated it. Myself. Eighteen months ago I couldn't hammer a nail in straight. That is an achievement, all that. And now, at the very end, she's trying to take it away from me, trying to cheat me of it.

Pause

Howard Come on Paul. You know, you've been fantastic. We both admire that. Can't you just relax and enjoy living here.

Paul No. I don't think I can.

Howard Well Marion's made up her mind, I've made up my mind.

Marion You're outvoted. You don't have an option.

Marion exits

Paul Yes I do. I can invoke the lease.

Howard You what?

Paul The lease. Tenants in Common. When one party wants to sell, everyone has to sell.

Howard Sell?

Paul Sell, yes. I want to sell my share of the flat.

Howard What? You're out of your mind. Haven't you noticed it's just got pleasant to live here. You don't take in a lungful of brickdust with your first morning fag. You don't find yourself halfway through a slash suddenly realizing some dickhead's moved the bog. We're living in *luxury* and you want to *sell*.

Paul I was going to wait till we'd done the kitchen. Next summer, maybe autumn. But if it's going to be in a sellable state in a couple of months, OK.

Howard OK what?

Paul Just . . . We can all make arrangements.

Howard Is this Ruth's idea?

Paul What?

Howard Has it got serious?

Paul Christ, Howie.

Howard I need to know, man, I'm in the fucking middle. A few months back I thought you were getting on with Marion again. I mean nobody actually tells me what's going on.

Paul Yeah. Well we did. Me and Marion. Just once. Well a few times. Nostalgia. It wasn't significant.

Howard Does she think it wasn't significant?

Paul It was nothing. But Ruth. It's hard to persuade her I'm still living with my ex-girlfriend and it's completely innocent.

Howard I can see her point.

Paul I get a lot of pressure. So all right. I'll sell up, at least it'll sort that part of my life out.

Howard Well where are you going to live? Doss down in her little cubby hole in Whitechapel?

Paul Possibly.

Howard Get married?

Paul Well it's a bit early for——

Howard What then?

There is a pause

Paul Well there's an idea I had at the back of my mind.

Howard Oh yeah?

Paul I was going to suggest it for next year. You wouldn't . . . You wouldn't fancy buying a house with me and Stewart would you?

There is a pause

See my share of this place would be what—forty-five. It's not a lot to play with. But with your share it's up to ninety. And Stewart's not happy, problems with his new woman. He's looking to sell. Pool it all, you're looking at a hundred and fifty K. It's a different league. There's still bits of Islington up for grabs, even some areas near Docklands. For that sort of money you could get hold of a good size Victorian house, three-storey, double-fronted. Need a bit doing to it, but in the long run you'd be looking at a very sizeable——

Howard Need what?

Paul Need . . . Need a bit doing to it.

Howard No.

Paul Stewart and I would do most of the work. Your bedroom first, it would be quick.

Howard No. I do not want to see another bag of cement as long as I live. I do not want to carry twenty foot lengths of knocked off timber along the street at the dead of night. I have sold my *Guardian* offer toolkit. Definitely no.

Paul Well what d'you want to do then. Because I'm selling. Which means you have to as well. And what can you do with your share? Forty grand'll get you fuck all in London. What you want to do, go back to Glasgow?

Marion enters carrying some bottles to put in the drinks cupboard

Marion I gave her a mugful of gin. It seems to be taking effect.

Paul (*quickly*) I agree.

Marion puts the bottles down

I think you're right. I think it's sensible. Let's get it done quickly.

Marion You've changed your mind.

Paul Yes.

Marion I think that's good. I really do.

Marion goes towards Paul to kiss him, but something stops her in her tracks

Paul And then as soon as the kitchen's done I want to sell. Because I don't like living here any more.

Marion Paul, you were the one who wanted to stay. All along. We only stayed because you insisted. Now you want to go. What's that about?

Paul Well. There's someone else in my life.

Howard I think I'll just see if Sherry's OK.

Howard exits

Marion So. It's to be Ruth. Ruth in Whitechapel, isn't that right?

Paul I . . .

There is a pause

Marion You don't have to apologize I'm not your wife. It's just—don't let us go around telling everyone what good *friends* we are when we don't even give each other the basic information. I bet she's got long hair.

Paul She has got long hair, yes.

Marion She has got long hair yes, what a breakthrough.

Paul I met her at a Style Council concert. Hammersmith Odeon, upstairs in the bar. It was truly horrible, everyone posing around, trying to look soulful. I was sticking my mike under people's noses trying to get some vox pops. Most of them refused because it wasn't television and their clothes wouldn't come over. Eventually I got round to her and she just said "I hate all these crappy people". I felt refreshed, I really did. I thought to myself, I don't have to stay here, I can be somewhere else with this girl. It was a moment of enlightenment. We went for a pizza. It was great.

Sherry enters wearing an old dressing-gown of Howard's. She is drinking gin from a coffee mug

Sherry Do you know the thing I discovered, the thing I *really* found out? The world is in a much better state then you'd expect. A much better state than you're led to believe.

Howard appears in the doorway, too late to stop Sherry

I mean, when you watch the news on television, you get so depressed, it's all wars and people blowing each other up, but when you actually get out there, in among it, it's not—you know—not such an awful planet after all. As planets go. I'm sorry, were you talking?

Marion Just you know, passing the time.

Howard Um, Sherry, I think your bath——

Sherry Oh God, I'd forgotten I put it on. Paul darling, you haven't got a clean towel have you, mine's in the wash.

Paul exits

Sherry follows Paul out

Howard tries to follow Sherry

Marion Howard.

Howard stops and turns

Paul hasn't offered you any sort of deal has he?

Howard He was talking. About maybe him and Stewart buying a place and me chipping in.

Marion What about this Ruth?

Howard She's still a student, she hasn't got any money.

Marion But she'd live there as well.

Howard I don't know, it's just an idea that's floating round.

Marion Is she nice?

Howard Only met her once. Good looking lass, doesn't say a lot.

Marion Bit boring, eh?

Howard I didn't say that.

Marion No. It's a relief for me that she's like that. There's no contest or anything. Only for his sake I wish she'd been someone more—you know challenging.

Howard Yeah.

Marion So he's serious. About selling up.

Howard I think he is, yes.

Marion considers this

Marion It's stupid to sell this place now. The boom's not stopping. The German banker on the top floor's selling, according to Claire, and he's gone on the market at a hundred and seventy-five. And he'll get it. OK, he's got planning permission to develop another storey, but even so, we can't be far behind.

Howard No.

Marion Do you want to buy a house with Paul?

Howard I don't know. (*Pause*) It's all wrong. People in the South. Us. Making a fortune out of flogging properties to each other. Who are we making a fortune from, that's the point? My mum's still in the same house she's been living in for the last forty years. That's not appreciating at twenty per cent a year, that's for sure. (*Pause*) He wants to buy somewhere and do it up. He's got the bug. I just don't want to live in all that rubble and disruption again.

Marion Then don't. Stay here. You keep your third. And I'll buy out Paul.

Howard Buy him out? You're talking about finding an extra forty-five grand.

Marion I can jack up my mortgage. I can borrow from Jeremy. And I can borrow from Claire.

Pause

Howard Christ.

Marion Remember all that hassle we had with Scott for a few thousand. All you have to do is sit in your room in this nice centrally-heated flat, and by this time next year you'll be worth another ten grand. You get the best of both worlds. It'll be quiet, you'll be able to write your book. No DIY. I work such long hours these days you'll have the place to yourself most of the time. You can use my word processor. And all the time you're getting richer. Now what's wrong with that? Mmmm?

Paul enters

Paul She's pissed already, I can't believe it.

Marion If you want to go, Paul, that's fine, I'll buy your share. As long as Howard doesn't want to go as well.

Paul Christ.

Marion Make a decision, Howard.

There is a pause

Howard I just ... I'm fed up with all the disruption. I don't want to move and start all over again. That's the reason I'm going to stay. That's the only reason.

Howard exits quickly

Paul goes to the french windows, and peers out

Paul I still can't believe we dug all that out, you know. It was six big skips. Full of rubble.

Marion holds him

Marion This is what you want, isn't it?
Paul Yeah. Yeah.

Sherry bursts in wearing only a bath towel and carrying a bottle of gin

Sherry Before I have my bath, I just want to say that I regret nothing. I am Edith Piaf. Got that?

Black-out

Music: "Fight for the Right (to Party)" by The Beastie Boys

SCENE 3

The same. May, 1987. Evening

The transformation of the room is now complete. It looks cool, refined and uncluttered—a few well-chosen objects in a big, open space

Stewart is lying on the floor, face up, head towards the back wall, fiddling with a radiator pipe

The French windows are open. Paul and Howard are standing outside. Howard is holding a large brown envelope, Paul a lengthy document word-processed on to A4. This is the manuscript of Howard's book

Stewart (*under the impression that Paul and Howard are in the room*) The argument that over one hundred and sixty thousand old people, all of them owner-occupiers, are projected to die in London in the course of nineteen eighty-eight and that, in consequence, an equal number of properties will come plonking on to the market, flooding demand and bringing the price of property down is at first sight a compelling one. (*Pause*) After all, Howard, everyone has a granny somewhere, and the mad stampede to get away, at all costs from said granny when she was a good deal younger and more socially useful than she is now, was a major factor in the property boom in the first place. So when Granny finally hands in her dinner pail, wouldn't one expect the nearest and dearest, doubtless a bunch of grasping bastards to a man, woman and child, to flog off the ancestral pile to the highest bidder and stuff the takings under their mattresses?

Paul and Howard enter through the french windows

Paul (*stuffing the manuscript in the envelope*) . . . and all the stuff about the city is great, the money markets——
Stewart Not so.

Paul and Howard stare at Stewart

The argument makes the fundamental error of over-estimating the ability of human beings to live in any kind of harmony with one another. The same impulse that caused son to abandon mother in the first place, i.e. the feeling that he couldn't stand the bitch, now impells him to leave his wife since he can now no longer stand that bitch either. So he returns to his now grannyless home with his new found doxy, leaving wife number one with her toy-boy in the house he's sweated away his life to buy. The number of available properties on the market remains constant. (*He sits up, wiping his hands*) So there you are. Just a compression joint. All it needed was a quick tighten up. Now, where did I put the bathroom?

He wanders off to wash his hands

Howard (*looking at Paul anxiously*) But, I mean overall—do you reckon it's any good?
Paul (*sitting*) It's great, of course it's good. I've just got one . . .
Howard (*sitting*) Yeah?
Paul The title.
Howard *The Myth of Recovery*. Do you not like that?
Paul *The Myth of Recovery*. You see, I think it's a bit chancy.
Howard What d'you mean?
Paul Well. Just supposing. Supposing the economic recovery isn't a myth, supposing there's some substance to it——
Howard But it is a myth. The book proves it's a myth. The dependence on

external factors like the valuation of the dollar and the price of commod-
ities and the short term buoyancy engendered by nationalized industry
sell-offs plus the end of the North Sea Oil bonanza means the so-called
Thatcherite recovery could be wiped out tomorrow if——

Paul But from a publisher's point of view. I mean it's saying something
people don't want to hear and it's sort of—speculative. I think that's why
you're having trouble getting it into print.

Howard So once the recovery has been clearly exposed as a fraud, it might
get published.

Paul Yes, I suppose.

Howard Only then—nobody'll have any money to spend on books.

Paul It won't be that bad.

Howard I think it will. That's my conclusion. We're about to hit the
downwave of a sixty-year cycle. Prices, wages, it's all going to start falling.
(*Reading*) "People in the North who are poor now will stay poor or
become poorer.

Stewart enters in time to pick up the drift

People in the South who are credit rich, theoretically rich, will find that
the dwindling value of the assets on which they've staked everything will
be far exceeded by the outgoings which are still paying for those very
assets." So in *real terms* they will be poor too.

Stewart Going to sell this place then, Howie?

Howard You what?

Stewart If I thought what you thought, I'd sell up. No point having a
mortgage in a downwave. Sell up and rent somewhere, that's what you
should do.

Howard (*standing*) Ah not this place, this is *central* London, man, it'll keep
its value——(*He leaves the manuscript on the table*)

Stewart Special factors eh?

Paul *Historical* factors——

Howard And we're still paying peanuts for it. At least I am.

Paul (*standing*) Up for the seven fifty-eight Stewart? We're a bit outclassed
here.

Stewart All right, young man.

Howard Bloody commuters, provincials.

Paul Nothing wrong with Greenwich, very fashionable.

Howard Apart from the fact you're in Charlton——

Paul Charltonish. It's nearer Greenwich though.

Howard Is it knackers!

Paul Oh listen. End of the month. At the Palladium. The Searchers are
playing their Silver Jubilee concert. D'you fancy coming? (*He gets out his
diary*)

Howard You have to hand it to them——

Paul Twenty-five years on the road——

Marion enters. She is carrying some candles for a table arrangement

Marion Oh.

Paul Just came by to pick up those tools.

Marion Oh. (*She starts to arrange the candles*)

Howard Stewart's fixed the leak.

Stewart Compression joint.

Paul Only we've got to be off. The train. That concert, Howie, it's the thirty-first.

Howard Put me down for it. Might be the last chance, you never know.

Paul (*watching Marion arrange the candles*) Nice.

Marion I've got some people coming round to dinner.

Howard Oh. Didn't see anything in the oven. Is it a microwave job?

Marion Having it delivered, silly.

Stewart Delivered, what, a dinner party?

Marion Three courses. A firm called Mr Sloane. Very good.

Stewart I'll make a note of the number.

Stewart exits. Howard follows Stewart out

Paul stands watching Marion

Marion I thought you were rushing off.

Paul I was just watching. Just for a moment.

Marion Is it working out?

Paul It's pretty good, yes.

Marion The three of you.

Paul Four. Stewart's new woman got a bit of cash out of her divorce so she bought a share. Makes it quite cheap.

Marion And how long will it take you to do it up?

Paul Couple of years. Maybe three. But it'll be all our own work. We start on the central heating next week.

Marion And the writing?

Paul Bits and pieces, you know. The music scene, you know, not a lot happening.

Marion Michael Jackson? Prince?

Paul Not a lot happening.

Marion And Ruth?

Paul Fine.

There is a pause

Marion Is it true?

Paul Yes. It's due in October.

Marion And you're happy about that.

Paul One of those things. You can't plan them really.

Marion No.

Paul The train.

He kisses her lightly on the check

Marion Telephone me. I'll take you to lunch sometime.

Paul Good. Yes. I've always liked lunch.

Howard enters

Paul thumps Howard on the shoulder

  Paul exits

Marion looks at the room and adjusts the lighting, using a dimmer switch

Howard Well.
Marion These people who are coming tonight——
Howard Yes. OK I'll keep out of the way.
Marion There's bound to be some food left over if you want to eat late.
Howard No. I'll go down the Hot Pot or something.

There is a pause

Marion I don't suppose I'll ever get to meet her.
Howard Well, she's a bit shy. Maybe when the baby's born.
Marion Why does he want to spend his life with someone who's shy? I just
  don't see that.
Howard She's a nice kid.

There is a pause

  Sherry was on the box again. I got it on the video for you.
Marion Oh.
Howard Did this stand-up monologue about roll-on deodorants. Magic.
  Audience were pissing themselves.
Marion Yes, she's doing so well.

The entryphone bleeps. Marion goes towards it

  Hello.

The entryphone crackles

  Yes, bring it through, will you. (*She turns back to Howard*) The food,
  thank Christ. If the guests arrive before the supper, the artifice is ruined.
Howard I'll get out of your way then. (*He sees his manuscript on the table*)
  I'll take this. (*He riffles the pages*) Might do a bit of tinkering with the
  chapter about the money supply.
Marion Great.

  Howard exits bashing the manuscript against his thigh

There is a pause

  A uniformed Deliverer enters, laden with bags. The Deliverer is Sherry

Deliverer Got yer scoff, lady, Gawd bless yer.

Marion turns

Marion Sherry. But——
Sherry I haven't let success go to my head. Yet. And it's a bit of steady
  money. Keeps me sober before I go onstage at ten.
Marion I——
Sherry Couldn't resist it when I saw your name on the list. The starters are

in this green bag. And the Salmis de Dinde à la Berrichonne's here. I'll put them in the kitchen on my way out. Do you want the gâteau in the fridge?

Marion Well, I suppose ... Yes.

Sherry And here's your aerosol.

Marion Aerosol?

Sherry It's a new touch. You waft it round the flat, it gives a general cooking smell. (*She sprays some in the air*) Nice, eh, this is the Paysanne flavour.

Marion You've only just missed Paul.

Sherry Oh. Shame. Still I see him a bit. He comes along and heckles me at the quiet venues. He's a good mate. Do you see him much?

Marion A bit. I'm very busy at the moment.

Sherry Great. And happy?

Marion It's really bizarre seeing you like this.

Sherry I'm happy. I'm having a great time. People point me out on the tube. Funny thing, though, if I've got this uniform on, nobody recognizes me. Good, eh? Howard walked straight past me in the corridor.

Marion I've seen you on the television. You've got very good. Much sharper.

Sherry After I came back. From the world tour. Things sort of fell into place for me. It all seemed so strange, this country. Cold, you know, emotionally cold. I just felt like grabbing hold of people and saying "Care. For fuck's sake, will you please care." So I just put that feeling into my act.

Marion And people laughed.

Sherry That's it. For the first time they laughed. Well better be off. Sign this. (*She offers Marion the chit*) Next drop's in Cheyne Walk, can't keep them waiting.

Marion signs the proffered chit

And this is your receipt, madam. I'll give Howard a cuddle on the way out. Take care.

They embrace for a moment. Sherry makes to go

Marion Sherry. Ring me.

Sherry Might well do. Or you could come and see me on the circuit. I'm better live. (*She looks around*) Nice place you've got here. (*She leaves one of the bags*)

Sherry exits

Marion sits. She opens the bag and looks at the food. She stands then pours a drink. She drinks and looks around for some moments

Music: the end of "Needles and Pins" fades in

Fade Lights

Music: "Needles and Pins" ends

Black-out

FURNITURE AND PROPERTY LIST

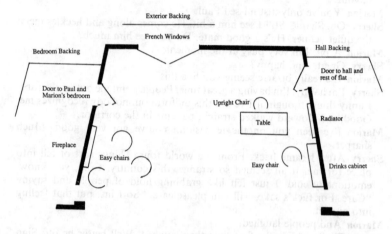

Exterior Backing

French Windows

Bedroom Backing

Hall Backing

Door to hall and
rest of flat

Door to Paul and
Marion's bedroom

Upright Chair

Table

Radiator

Fireplace

Easy chairs

Easy chair

Drinks cabinet

ACT I

Scene 1

On stage: Table. *On it:* typewriter, books, papers, card index systems and pens, etc.
Drinks cupboard. *In it:* bottle of brandy, bottle of sherry and glasses. *On it:* ornaments
Pictures on the walls
Upright chair
Easy chairs
Cassette machine: practical
Carpet
Curtains
Fireplace. *On it:* ornaments
Radiator
Dimmer switch
Further dressing may be added at the director's discretion

Off stage: Huge shoulder bag **(Sherry)**
Car keys **(Paul)**
Cassette tape with prerecorded interview **(Paul)**
Tray. *On it:* traditional earthenware teapot, four distinctive mugs, a bottle of milk, a sugar bowl and a packet of biscuits **(Marion)**

Personal: **Sherry:** absurd floppy hat
Howard: ten pound note

SCENE 2

On stage:	As before
Set:	Small, genuine Christmas tree with working lights Hoover: practical Christmas cards adorn every available surface
Strike:	Tray. *On it:* traditional earthenware teapot, four distinctive mugs, a bottle of milk, a sugar bowl and a packet of biscuits
Off stage:	Briefcase. *In it:* papers **(Anthony Scott)** Micro tape recorder **(Anthony Scott)**
Personal:	**Anthony Scott:** watch, business card

SCENE 3

On stage:	As before
Set:	Microphone Cardboard boxes. *In them:* some of the books, ornaments and pictures from the previous scenes
Strike:	Christmas tree Hoover Christmas cards
Off stage:	Four empty cardboard boxes **(Marion)**

SCENE 4

On stage:	As before
Strike:	Cardboard boxes A number of ornaments, etc. to make the room appear a little emptier
Off stage:	Mug of coffee **(Sherry)** Large brown envelope. *In it:* a number of twenty pound notes and one ten pound note **(Marion)** Tray. *On it:* four glasses and a bottle of champagne **(Paul)** Yale key **(Sherry)**
Personal:	**Anthony Scott:** watch

ACT II

SCENE 1

Set:	Huge dust cloth to cover the floor
Strike:	All furniture and property fittings, including the carpet and curtains
Off stage:	Large plastic dustbin. *In it:* rubble **(Howard** and **Paul)** Expensive-looking carrier bag from Next **(Marion)** Empty plastic dustbin **(Stewart)** Postcard **(Paul)** Large plastic dustbin. *In it:* rubble **(Howard** and **Stewart)**

Estate agent's "For Sale" sign mounted on a seven foot length of three by two (**Stewart**)
Two estate agents' signs (**Howard**)
Estate agent sign and an empty bin (**Stewart**)

Personal: **Howard:** cigarettes

SCENE 2

Set: New curtains
              Wooden floor
              Large rolled rug wrapped in thick brown paper and tied with cord in the middle of the floor
              Delivery docket on the mantelpiece
              Sleeping bag
              Rucksack. *In it:* clothes etc.
              Black holdall

Strike: Dust cloth
              Estate agents' signs
              Postcard

Off stage: Small cardboard box (**Paul**)
              Plant (**Marion**)
              New drinks cabinet (**Marion**)
              Drinks bottles (**Marion**)
              Mug. *In it:* gin (**Sherry**)
              Bottle of gin (**Sherry**)

Personal: **Howard:** cigarette
              Paul: Swiss Army knife

SCENE 3

Set: A few well-chosen objects to reflect the complete transformation of the room, including chairs and a table
              Entryphone
              Large brown envelope (for **Howard**)
              Glasses in drinks cabinet
              Lengthy A4 word-processed document (for **Paul**)
              Open French windows

Strike: Small cardboard box
              Sleeping bag
              Rucksack
              Black holdall
              Delivery docket

Off stage: Candles (**Marion**)
              Bags (one of them green). *In them:* food containers, aerosol (**Sherry**)

Personal: **Paul:** diary
              Sherry/Deliverer: delivery chit

LIGHTING PLOT

Property fittings required: Christmas tree lights for Act I, Scene 2

Interior: a sitting room. The same scene throughout

ACT I, Scene 1.   Just before midnight

To open: General interior lighting. Dark exterior lighting for backdrop
to French windows

Cue 1   **Frank:** "And Marshall Crenshaw came to see us in New   (Page 9)
York . . ."
Quick fade to black-out

ACT I, Scene 2.   Evening

To open: General interior lighting. Dark exterior lighting for backdrop
to French windows. Christmas tree lights on

Cue 2   **Marion:** ". . . Until he does."   (Page 17)
Quick fade to black-out

ACT I, Scene 3

To open: General interior lighting. General exterior lighting for backdrop to French windows

Cue 3   **Marion:** (*off*) Sherry!   (Page 25)
Quick black-out

ACT I, Scene 4.   Morning, around eleven o'clock

To open: General interior lighting. Bright exterior lighting for backdrop
to French windows

Cue 4   **Sherry:** "I've got such a lot to do."   (Page 33)
Quick black-out

ACT II, Scene 1.   Early afternoon

To open: General interior lighting. Bright and sunny exterior lighting for
backdrop to French windows

Cue 5   **Stewart:** "The web of Wyrd."   (Page 42)
Black-out

ACT II, Scene 2.   Early evening

To open: General interior lighting. Dusk exterior lighting for backdrop
            to French windows

Cue 6   **Sherry:** "Got that?"   (Page 52)
          Black-out

ACT II, Scene 3.   Evening

To open: General interior lighting. Dusk exterior lighting for backdrop
            to French windows

Cue 7   **Marion** adjusts the lighting, using the dimmer switch   (Page 56)
          Reduce general lighting

Cue 8   Music: the end of "Needles and Pins" fades in   (Page 57)
          Fade lights

Cue 9   Music: "Needles and Pins" ends   (Page 57)
          Black-out

EFFECTS PLOT

ACT I

Cue 1	To open SCENE 1 *Music: "Needles and Pins" by the Searchers*	(Page 1)
Cue 2	The Lights come up *Fade music*	(Page 1)
Cue 3	Fade to Black-out *Music: "When You Walk in the Room" by the Searchers*	(Page 9)
Cue 4	**Paul:** "... and we don't want Sherry saying anything." *Sound of the front door opening and closing*	(Page 9)
Cue 5	**Sherry:** "Depressed, right." *Doorbell*	(Page 10)
Cue 6	**Sherry:** "I'm breaking into the alternative comedy scene." *Sound of the front door opening and closing*	(Page 12)
Cue 7	Quick fade to Black-out *Music: "I Don't Like Mondays" by the Boomtown Rats*	(Page 17)
Cue 8	**Marion:** "We've got an early start." *Telephone rings in the hall*	(Page 22)
Cue 9	**Marion** exits to answer the telephone *Cut telephone*	(Page 22)
Cue 10	Black-out *Music: "Money for Nothing" by Dire Straits*	(Page 25)
Cue 11	**Howard:** "And so do you." *Doorbell*	(Page 26)
Cue 12	**Sherry:** "... I had no idea it was so expensive—" *Doorbell*	(Page 30)

ACT II

Cue 13	To open SCENE 1 *Music: "You Can Call Me Al" by Paul Simon*	(Page 34)
Cue 14	Black-out *Music: "Don't Leave Me This Way" by the Communards*	(Page 42)
Cue 15	**Howard:** "Never has any cash these days." *Sound of the front door shutting*	(Page 44)
Cue 16	Black-out *Music: "Fight for the Right (to Party)" by The Beastie Boys*	(Page 52)

Cue 17	**Marion:** "Yes, she's doing so well."	(Page 56)
	Entryphone bleeps	
Cue 18	**Marion:** "Hello."	(Page 56)
	Entryphone crackles	
Cue 19	**Marion** drinks and looks around for some moments	(Page 57)
	Music: the end of "Needles and Pins" fades in	
Cue 20	Fade Lights	(Page 57)
	Music: "Needles and Pins" ends	

A licence issued by Samuel French Ltd to perform this play does NOT include permission to use any copyright music in the performance. The notice printed below on behalf of the Performing Right Society should be carefully read.

The following statement concerning the use of music is printed here on behalf of the Performing Right Society Ltd, by whom it was supplied
The permission of the owner of the performing right in copyright music must be obtained before any public performance may be given, whether in conjunction with a play or sketch or otherwise, and this permission is just as necessary for amateur performances as for professional. The majority of copyright musical works (other than oratorios, musical plays and similar dramatico-musical works) are controlled in the British Commonwealth by the PERFORMING RIGHT SOCIETY LTD, 29–33 BERNERS STREET, LONDON W1P 4AA.

The Society's practice is to issue licences authorizing the use of its repertoire to the proprietors of premises at which music is publicly performed, or alternatively, to the organizers of musical entertainments, but the Society does not require payment of fees by performers as such. Producers or promoters of plays, sketches, etc., at which music is to be performed, during or after the play or sketch, should ascertain whether the premises at which their performance are to be given are covered by a licence issued by the Society, and if they are not, should make application to the Society for particulars as to the fee payable.

MADE AND PRINTED IN GREAT BRITAIN BY
LATIMER TREND & COMPANY LTD, PLYMOUTH
MADE IN ENGLAND